FRIENDS
FOREVER

FRIENDS FOREVER

Edited by
RANDAL A. WRIGHT

Bookcraft
Salt Lake City, Utah

Library of Congress Catalog Card Number: 96-84348
ISBN 1-57008-243-X

First Printing, 1996

Printed in the United States of America

CONTENTS

1

FRIENDS AND FRIENDSHIP

Richard Neitzel Holzapfel

For many teenagers (and as parents will agree), the adolescent years can be both a rewarding and a challenging period. During this stage of life, the physical body begins to change in dramatic and profound ways. Just as we may think we know who we are and what our place is in the world, we go through a series of growth spurts that change our height, our complexion, and, for young men, our voice. Physically, our bodies begin to look like those of full-grown adults.

During my ten years of teaching seminary and institute for the Church Educational System in Irvine, California, it was not unusual to have young men in my classes who looked more adult than I did. Some of them could grow a beard if they wanted to, whereas I still could not grow one! Even though some of my students looked like adults, for the most part they still lacked the experiences most adults share—experiences that come only with time.

During junior high and high school years, young men and young women continue to grow physically, emotionally, socially, and spiritually. In time, the emotional and spiritual person inside the adult body catches up with the physical body. During this critical period of a young person's development, friends play a decisive role in gaining the experiences that teach one to act and think completely as an adult.

The dictionary defines a friend as someone attached to another by affection or esteem. In this context, a friend could be a parent or sibling, a school associate, a member of the Church or a nonmember, someone of the same or opposite gender, a schoolteacher or coach, a local Church leader or a General Authority, or, of course, the Lord.

Before we reach our first years of school experience, most of our friends are family members and a few neighborhood children or Primary classmates. As we continue to associate with peers at school and church, our circle of friends increases to include a much larger group. By the time we enter junior high and high school, our friendships include a host of diverse people, including teachers and coaches and youth leaders at church. By the end of our high school experience, our circle of friends includes a great variety of people of different ages and backgrounds.

We naturally want positive and healthy friendships. For some people, whether young or old, happiness is a social calendar packed with activities involving lots of friends. For others, it's having lots of uninterrupted free time to spend with a small circle of friends or even one best friend.

I remember a song that was popular when I was just out of high school, one line of which stated: "Thank you for being my friend." I recall very clearly my feelings when this hit song played on the radio. I thought about my friends and, in particular, about one close friend. I realized how much I enjoyed my association with a circle of people who were very important to me. Such feelings are right and natural.

Sociability of any kind, whether in large or small groups, is worth cultivating. According to my own experience, people need and expect to have friends. Our friendships can make us healthier, happier, and better able to cope with the stresses of life's challenges.

A healthy balance of several types of friends that include a broad cross section of people from several groups—such as family, school, church, and others—ensures a safety net as we proceed on the exciting journey of life. These friendships allow us to be remarkably resistant to the emotional and physical ills that are common to the human experience.

Our friendships can have a lasting impact on our life both here in mortality and in the world to come. Throughout our mortal life, friends will come and go—a natural consequence of the fast-paced and highly mobile world in which we live. From the time I was five years of age until I graduated from high school, my family moved six times because of my father's naval career. Moving from Idaho to Hawaii, then to Northern California, to Hawaii, to Maine, to Southern California, and then to Maine again had its challenges. It is difficult to find friends and spend the time necessary to cultivate friendships in such situations. Nevertheless, I did have good friends, some of whom I still have contact with today.

Even if I had not moved so often, I suppose that some friends would have been closer to me than others at times. As we grow, we each develop new interests and have new opportunities, which allows us to meet wonderful people at a new job, in a new school class, or in a new church setting. Of all these friendships, some are much more important than others. We must always put things in proper perspective: All friends are not equal, nor should they be.

Home is the primary and most influential place where we can find friends and develop long-lasting friendships. More important, home is the best place to learn about friendship and to develop the necessary skills for being a good friend. Whether parents or siblings, family friends can become lifetime friends with whom we will spend holiday seasons and attend special celebrations such as baptisms, graduations, missionary farewells, and marriages. Family friends will also come together at difficult times, such as the death of a family member. As I grow older, my family friends continue to play a significant role in my life, while my best friends from high school play a smaller role today.

Nothing is wrong with having close relationships with school and church friends in high school and college, but we must remember that in reality those relationships are often only temporary. When I think about the many friends I shared time with in high school and college, only a few still remain close to me. Although I fondly remember them, I nevertheless have developed stronger relationships with my own wife and my five children. By and large, my high school and college friends and I have moved on in our lives, some to faraway places. For the most part, we have established meaningful relationships with people we did not know in high school and college. Even though I live far away from my parents' home in Missouri and from two sisters who live in California and Texas, we have contact more often than I do with most of my high school and college friends. Why? Because the family usually continues to play a significant role in our adult lives.

That is why it is so important to develop friendships with our own parents and siblings. Although we will still have traditional child-parent and sibling relationships, it is much more meaningful to enjoy friend-to-friend relationships with family members. Parents and children need to do things that develop friendly relationships as much as child-parent and sibling relationships.

Surely parents want their children to feel comfortable in the basic family unit of the Church and of society at large. Yet, like most parents, I want my children to explore and gain experiences outside the walls of our home. My own children, who range in age from six to sixteen, are finding friends beyond our family circle. It is not only natural for them to make new friends and spend time with their friends, but this process is essential as they come to know themselves and develop the skills that will be necessary to making lasting relationships in the future.

Although I am somewhat saddened that my children are progressively reaching the point when they will be cutting the apron strings, I rejoice that they are energetic in confronting the world with all the enthusiasm and idealism so representative of young people in the Church today. This is truly an exciting time to be alive!

As a teacher at Brigham Young University, I am able to see many bright smiles and looks of expectation as young people—some only seventeen or eighteen years of age—enter my classroom. For many, college is their first experience away from home, from the friendly surroundings of a local high school, from a community they know well, and from a church setting they feel comfortable with. Their first semester at the university is full of hopes and promises. They spread their wings to fly and see the world on their own for the first time. However, I also see their frustrations as they attempt to fit in and find friends. Some feel homesick for their family, school, and church friends back home. The leap from the familiar to a larger world is often overwhelming.

For many of my students, the first year away from home allows them to become more mature and thus more independent—which is exactly what most parents really desire for their children. This growing gives strength and adds character. It also allows young people to appreciate their friends at home—especially their family friends. Sometimes absence does make the heart grow fonder!

My first year of college was when I truly discovered that good friends are an essential ingredient for a wonderful and rich life. Choosing the right friends is one of the most important decisions a person makes. Good friends support us during times of discouragement and trial; good friends bring the best out in us; and good friends never demand that we prove our friendship.

The biggest trap teenagers face may be that of proving their friendship or love by doing something they do not feel good about or something that is against their standards. If associates ask us to prove our friendship or our love, we can know that they do not have our best interests in mind and that they have the wrong idea about what it means to be a friend.

As a freshman at college, I found several good friends. Being around them made me want to be the best I could be, whether in my schoolwork or on the basketball court. They always supported me in making decisions that were good for me. One particular friend, a returned missionary who was from Southern California, helped me make a choice to serve a mission—but not by arguing or putting a guilt trip on me. His example spoke louder than any sermon. He supported me in making the right decision when I did not necessarily have the support of others. Luckily, I have had the opportunity since then to thank him for his kindness and support during a very critical period of my life. I realized then that the Lord was concerned about the friends I chose and that making the right choice in friends made a difference in my life.

Interestingly, the scriptures talk a lot about friends and friendship. The Bible, the Book of Mormon, the Doctrine and Covenants, and the Pearl of Great Price contain literally hundreds of references on this subject.

Jesus put friendship in proper perspective when he said: "Greater love hath no man than this, that a man lay down his life for his *friends*" (John 15:13; emphasis added). Later, he told his disciples that he was their friend: "Ye are my *friends*" (John 15:14; emphasis added). Of course, Jesus' love for his disciples and for us is demonstrated by the fact that he did "lay down his life for his friends."

In the Book of Mormon we read of the sadness and loneliness a person can feel when he or she cannot find a good and loyal friend. Following the destruction of the Nephite people,

Moroni wandered in the wilderness. He wrote: "I am alone. My father hath been slain in battle, and all my kinsfolk, and I have not *friends* nor whither to go" (Mormon 8:5; emphasis added).

Making good friendships with family, school, church, and neighborhood individuals is often challenging. Everyone struggles to find and maintain satisfactory relationships. I have learned that I can go through all the motions of being a friend and still feel distant from those around me. Without genuine concern, associations in our families, at school, and at church can seem hollow.

A significant part of growing up includes acquiring the skills of friendship. These skills are like the tools a carpenter uses to build a house. Without knowing what tools are needed, a person could never build a comfortable home. However, even knowing what tools are used in the construction of a house is not sufficient; we must also know how to use these tools.

The "how" comes by experience, which begins in our small circle of friends as young children, especially within our own homes. Experience is the best teacher; yet if we can learn from the experiences of others, the cost in terms of time and pain is much less.

At first, we need to think about developing friendships and defining what kind of friend we want to be. As already mentioned, we all naturally want and expect to have friends. At the same time, each of us should expect to be a friend to others. Learning to be a good friend may sound mechanical, but it is necessary if we want to gain the skills of friendship.

When I was living in Southern California as a fifteen-year-old, I began to learn how to drive. My first few experiences of driving on the freeway and learning to parallel park on a hill were difficult. I remember clutching the steering wheel tightly and feeling the intensity build as I pulled from the on-ramp into the main flow of traffic on the San Diego freeway for the first time. Today, however, I rarely feel that way. I hardly think about the skills of driving now, but I did then. Developing friendships does take skills. Even if we are naturally outgoing, we must take the next step in developing this strength to become a good friend. Everyone can learn and perfect the skills of friendship.

Some of the basic skills of friendship include the ability to apologize, be courteous, encourage wholesomeness, be fair in our expectations, forgive, be friendly, give of ourselves, honor others in our speech, and, most important, be loyal.

These nine skills of friendship are essential ingredients to good relationships with any type of friend. However, I do not suggest that we cannot have friends without knowing these nine skills by name. Many of us naturally use many of these skills in our lives already. Learning the skills of friendship by name and recognizing why they are important are quite simple activities, but learning to use all the skills can be a slow and agonizing process.

Certainly, people can survive and go through life without developing friendship skills, but such people are often part of what I call our modern jungle society. Members of the jungle society have developed a form of behavior that helps them survive at home, at school, or at church. They may feel safe in those environments and they may feel in control, but their methods of surviving do not allow them to develop quality friendships. Most of us know these types of people; they have so-called friends because they are popular, have money, are a sports hero, or manipulate people through their physical size or through verbal intimidation. When these jungle-society members become adults and get married, they often spend much of their time wondering why their relationships are not healthy and positive. They usually blame others for their problems.

I remember one case involving a certain person who moved into our ward. A few months later he told me how disappointed he was in the ward. "No one has been friendly," he stated forcibly. I felt bad because truly, ward members should reach out to welcome everyone. This does not mean that we must be best friends with everyone, but we should be friendly and courteous to everyone no matter what.

I asked this new ward member what had happened to make him feel the way he felt. In his case, it was what did not happen that mattered. "No one has ever invited me to dinner or to any activities," he responded. I apologized for the ward as the bishop, but then I asked two very difficult questions: "Whom have *you* invited to your home? Whom have *you* invited to go with you to an activity?" He thought about my questions briefly and then confessed, "No one." To want friends is one thing, but it is another thing to be a friend.

Learning to be a good friend has tremendous value for any young man or young woman, not only now but also later in life. Many young people will live with roommates. Often, roommates come from different backgrounds and experiences. Friend-shipping skills can make college experiences more positive and rewarding.

A missionary spends twenty-four hours a day with a companion. The skills of friendship help make missionary service more productive and fun. Two of my good friends today were missionaries in Switzerland and Italy, where I served. They have demonstrated the skills of friendship, and as a result we have continued to make the effort to keep in contact, developing our friendship as we share life's experiences together. All three of us married in the temple, have children, and continue to be active in the Church—all of which are blessings that come from willingness to serve the Lord in the mission field.

Finally, the skills of friendship can make our marriages stronger and more positive. Individuals who learn and use the skills of friendship are more successful in their marriages and have many more positive and rewarding personal experiences. Perhaps the best advice anyone could give a young person who is preparing for marriage is to find someone who can be his or her best friend. This friendship must then be continually cultivated throughout the marriage. It is truly a blessing to be married to your best friend.

The experiences of high school and college dating provide

necessary building blocks for our future family life. These experiences are important and necessary. Although not all our dating experiences will be remembered fondly, they can teach us about being friends with someone. Learning from such experiences is a reward that can help us for the rest of our lives.

I say without reservation that if the people you date or spend time with as friends are not treating you kindly and do not try to develop the skills mentioned above, they are not your real friends. Do not accept anything less in your relationships. Everyone is entitled to kind treatment and loyalty.

The chapters in this book explore the nature and importance of friends and friendship among the groups and types of friends we should have as we live life to its fullest. Each contributor shares experiences and counsel from his or her own life. We can learn from others, as already mentioned. The wonderful youth leaders and teachers who have contributed to this volume are ready to share their experiences about friends and friendship. They are good friends because they truly want the best for us and want us to be truly happy.

Richard Neitzel Holzapfel, *an assistant professor in Church History and Doctrine at Brigham Young University, is an award-winning author and popular speaker. He and his wife, Jeni, and their five children live in Woodland, Utah.*

2

BEING FRIENDS
WITH YOURSELF

Matt Richardson

I t has been years since I looked through my junior high and high school yearbooks. It was fun to think back upon so many memories recalled by a glance of a single picture. Although it seems like only yesterday, the pictures and styles attest that it wasn't. I am finding it nearly impossible to convince my family (or anyone else for that matter) that the clothes I was wearing and my hairstyle were actually really cool back in those days.

While the styles and activities have changed, one thing in my yearbook hasn't gone out of style. I'm not talking about the sports, clubs, academics, music, or the endless rows of student and faculty pictures (a cross between mug shots and those not-so-flattering pictures on a driver's license that make you want to laugh, scream, or feel pity). What I am talking about are all the scribbles of pen, pencil, or marker over the pictures, in the creases, and on the inside covers—the signatures of my peers. It seems that autographing yearbooks is one thing that has remained in vogue.

I still remember poring over my yearbook at the conclusion of each school year and feeling relief when I cracked open the cover to discover that someone had actually written in it. For some odd reason, it seemed that my concept of friends was somehow tied to my yearbook. In a way, a yearbook was actually a friendship report card, the telltale proof at the conclusion of a school year that you either had friends or you didn't. After rereading those once-cherished notations made by my peers, I have determined that it couldn't be the quality of the inscriptions that characterized friendship. I found dozens that said "You're a great guy. Whatever you do, don't change!" or "I'm really glad I got to know you this year" or "Come and see me sometime" or the safe and reliable "Have a fun summer" or my all-time favorite, "Call me sometime." Most of these meaningful inscriptions were followed by the signature of Pam, Jeff, Kurt, or some other first name; most of the signatures in my yearbooks don't include a last name! I even found a couple of inscriptions simply signed "Me!" *Me?* Who in the world is *Me?*

I finally came across an inscription that explained my connection between friendship and yearbooks. It went something like this: "You must be so popular—I can't even find a spot to write in your yearbook." There it is! Obviously it really doesn't matter what people write; what really matters is how many people write in your yearbook. It seems that for far too many of us, the validation of friendship hinges upon the number of friends, as one can plainly count in a yearbook.

Perhaps the rationale goes something like this: The more signatures my yearbook contains, the more friends I have. The more friends I have, the more I am liked. The more I am liked by others, the more I should be able to like myself—after all, all those friends can't be wrong! Now, you may be chuckling, thinking that surely this doesn't apply to you. You may not even have a yearbook. This problem, however, is broader than mere signatures in a yearbook.

If we aren't worrying about the number of signatures in a yearbook, then we are probably worrying about dating. Those of us who actually do go on dates are probably worrying whether we go on enough dates. And those who date a lot are probably worrying about not going on the dream date. It's a vicious cycle that involves clothing, the number of times someone has said hi to them, invitations to parties, money, grade point averages, batting averages, and the list goes on and on and on! For some reason, when most of us think of friendship, we think of others or of things that, as Elder Neal A. Maxwell has said, "demand extrinsic evidence" (*Meek and Lowly* [Salt Lake City: Deseret Book Co., 1987], p. 48). Such evidence is generally tangible and therefore countable. Thus we fall into the trap of thinking that more is obviously better.

In all of my memorabilia from my high school days, there is one inscription that stands out above all the rest. As a matter of fact, I would be completely satisfied if this was the only thing written in each yearbook every year for the rest of my life. "One inscription? Are you crazy?" you might ask. How can you face life with only one signature? What does that tell anyone who picks up your yearbook and starts thumbing through: that you have only one friend? What type of future lies in store for a person whose yearbook isn't marked up with smiling faces, exclamation points, markers, pens, and home-grown art? Nevertheless, I would still trade it all for that one inscription.

This single inscription that made such an impact on me was actually a small handwritten note on a half-sheet of paper. Although it was written during the first half of my senior year, I actually received it in the mail a few years after I graduated from high school. It started off, "Dear Matt." It contained a few detailed plans for the future, feelings about school, and some hopes as well as concerns. But the part that I found so satisfying was the ending: "Hang in there, you're OK. Your Friend, Matt."

You might question why I would think that this inscription

alone could replace all those other signatures in my yearbook, why this little note would give me a better understanding and feeling about friends and friendship than all the rest of those inscriptions. Let me explain. This note was written by me! This letter was actually an assignment from one of my classes. My classmates and I were required to write a letter to ourselves. Several years later, our teacher mailed our assignments. What a blast from the past! I laughed at some of the contents in that letter, but I was touched by the closing lines: "Your Friend, Matt."

Hopefully you can understand why I would trade "Have a fun summer" written by someone that I haven't seen in years with a "You're OK. Your Friend, Matt" from someone who has been there during every moment of my life since graduation: me! While I believe that friendship with others is important and even vital, real friendship is more than having friends who can sum up all the years of knowing you in a sentence or two in a school yearbook. Real friendship doesn't require ten, sixty, or one thousand friends. It doesn't require proof, things, or extrinsic validations. This may sound a little odd, but you can have a million friends and still be lonely. Real friendship is determined not by how many friends we count, but by whom we start counting as our friends.

Not long ago I was marveling at my seven-year-old daughter. She has a gleam in her eye that I have envied for years; she must have inherited it from my wife. This little girl views life in a remarkable manner. Megan came out of our bathroom once after combing her hair and exclaimed, "Aren't I beautiful?" I knew immediately that she wasn't fishing for a compliment, nor was she being proud. She was expressing a heartfelt statement of fact. I responded with a big smile and said, "Yes, Megan, you are beautiful!" Perhaps I was hoping that by acknowledging Megan's beauty, I might also be acknowledging her dad's genes at work! Truth be known, Megan's inner beauty, as well as her outer beauty, is a testimony of my wife's genes at work . . . again!

That wasn't the only time Megan exhibited this wonderful confidence. She does it when she says her prayers at night, blessing everyone—including herself. For example, she did it once during our weekly family night. Every family home evening, one family member has a turn to bear his or her testimony. We feel that bearing our testimonies to each other is just as important as giving a lesson or singing a song. It happened to be Megan's turn. She stood in front of our family and with that wonderful inner confidence said, "I love my mom and dad and Zachary and Lauren and myself." I marveled at how easily she said it: "I love myself." When Megan speaks of her friends, she talks about Robert, Jennifer, Zach, Lauren, many others, and Megan—that's right, Megan. This wonderfully confident little girl and my yearbook letter have taught me a vital lesson about friendship: The secret to meaningful friendship is being friends with yourself.

When I think of Megan's friendship with herself, I can't help but think of a line written in a term paper by one of my former students: "The day we are born, we are showered with love from every imaginable source. It only goes downhill from there." I have heard life's complaints from those who are suffering from a mid-life crisis or another year over the hill, but this was the first time I had ever heard that life gets worse immediately after you leave the hospital delivery room. "Live it up while you can," a first-grader may say to a kindergartner at recess. "The thrill is gone when you get to be my age!" I shudder to think that perhaps liking yourself or being your own friend is something that you will just grow out of. It's scary to think that it's just a matter of time before you'll be alone. This seems especially unfair considering that the time you need a friend most is as you grow older and life gets more complicated.

Sister Joanne B. Doxey, former second counselor in the Relief Society general presidency, gives hope that self-friendship can last. She said, "Individual worth is intrinsic; it is internal; it is eternal. It is something that cannot be taken from us when the blossom of youth fades, when economic conditions leave us desolate, when sickness or handicaps befall us, or when prominence and visibility are obscured." ("Strengthening the Family," *Ensign,* November 1987, p. 91.) I love this statement. When we find a friend within ourselves, nobody, no thing, no comment (regardless of how cruel), and no bout of loneliness can take away that friend. You won't outgrow it, you can't buy it, and it isn't based on recognition, but apparently you can decide to abandon it. *You* decide. This idea is sharply different from external validations. But is maintaining self-friendship a guarantee of happiness and security? What about those who have already come to realize their faults, shortcomings, and failures and have begun to lose self-friendship or become their own worst enemy? Can they find that confidence again? There are a few things all of us can try.

Change Your Perspective

A few years ago my wife and I had the opportunity to visit Switzerland. As we traveled through a beautiful area connected by several lakes, I honestly felt that the scenery couldn't possibly get any better. When we arrived at the city center, we were told that a series of train connections could take us to the top of the Jungfrau, one of the Alps surrounding the region. The drawback, however, was the expense. Tickets for both my wife and me would cost several hundred dollars, quite a price to pay for a different perspective! I remember squinting as I looked to the top of the Alps and then looking around at the area. It seemed that I could see everything just fine from where I was standing—and closer-up too. I had the hardest time imagining that this beauty could be any better just because we were higher up.

We decided that this might be our only visit to Switzerland, so we bought our tickets. At first there wasn't much of a difference as we left the city. With each passing mile, however, the scenery was not only more beautiful but it was different. As we ascended to the top of the Jungfrau, the view became more and more breathtaking. I will never forget the incredible difference I witnessed as I stood on an observation deck at the top of the Jungfraujoch with my wife. Not only was the view beautiful but it was immense. I couldn't believe how far I could see, how clear everything was, and how much more there was to this region than a few lakes and a couple of mountains. I was embarrassed to think that we almost missed this experience because we thought we could see everything from the bottom. A change in perspective helped me see a whole new world!

While most of us will never be confronted with a decision to take a train up a mountain, we all must face the decision of how we will view ourselves. When you take a look at yourself, what do you see? I believe that what you see depends upon your perspective. If you view yourself from the base of the mountain, from the perspective that nearly everyone has, you will find a view of yourself that is filled with flaws, faults, and inadequacies. From this vantage point, it is easy to remember all the failures and hardships. A change in your perspective will change what you see and feel and how you act.

Perhaps the challenge of being friends with yourself is to not remember failures, mistakes, and other problems. Possibly the difficulty comes from concentrating on the wrong things. As we fail to measure up to the standards placed before us, we usually assume that we are failures. Once again, it is the perspective that defines failure, not the performance. Sister Elaine L. Jack, Relief Society general president, suggested that in such moments you ask yourself, "Are the comparisons you may make of yourself and others based on the model of the Savior's life, or do they come from trying to fit your life into the pattern of others' lives?" ("These Things Are Manifested unto Us Plainly," *Ensign,* November 1990, p. 89.) Such comparisons can be overwhelming, not to mention dangerous. With so many expectations from the world, how can anyone measure up completely today? Elder James E. Faust has reminded us that the standards most of us use to measure worth and value are inadequate. He inquired, "Have we been measuring by standards that are too short and unworthy of those in the pursuit of holiness?" ("The Dignity of Self," *Ensign,* May 1981, p. 9.)

Any friendship, with self or others, will unravel if all of our energies are spent finding faults, weaknesses, and those irritating little quirks. How long do you think you would want to be with someone who constantly belittles others with reminders of not measuring up, that one ear is bigger than the other, or of the failures of the past? While we couldn't imagine doing that to others, we feel that we have full right to do it to ourselves. How different would the world be if we changed the Golden Rule to "do unto others as we do unto ourselves"? Ouch! What most people don't realize is that when we view life from the base of the mountain, we see the base elements of life. No wonder most of us don't see good in ourselves: from our vantage point, it is not only difficult to see anything good, it is almost impossible to imagine ourselves any other way.

Find Balance in Friendship

A lawyer once asked Jesus Christ, "Master, which is the great commandment in the law?" Jesus responded by saying, "Thou shalt love the Lord thy God with all thy heart, and with all thy soul, and with all thy mind. This is the first and great commandment. And the second is like unto it, Thou shalt love thy neighbour as thyself." (Matthew 22:35–39.) It seems the Master taught that there are four components required in true friendship: love, God, self, and others. The combination of these four elements of friendship develops the kind of friendship that Sister Doxey said "cannot be taken from us."

As I think back to those yearbook days, friendship was so fragile. You could find that your best friend suddenly decided not to be your friend at all. In light of Christ's teachings, perhaps friendship's fragility is due to its excessive emphasis on others. Too many of us try to fool ourselves into believing that if we have enough "others" in our lives, we can escape the need for being friends with ourselves. However, no matter how many signatures are penned in your yearbook, or dates you have been on, or buddies you have, or things you acquire, the peace and comfort of real friendship—lasting friendship—can never be felt if you are missing any one of friendship's four components. It really doesn't matter which one you don't include. If you spend a lifetime in the service of God, for example, but fail to nurture friendship with others, you will miss the full measure of true friendship. I believe that Christ was very clear and very precise in teaching all of us true friendship. It must include all four elements: love, God, self, and others.

See as God and Christ See

As we climb the Lord's mountain, we find not only the power of eternity but also eternal perspective. I am often amused by some of the things children say in their testimonies and prayers. Statements such as "I'd like to *bury* my testimony" or "I know my mom and dad are true" have always made me chuckle. I remember when a child once tried to start a prayer by addressing our Father in Heaven in a rather grown-up manner: "O God, the *Internal* Father." *Whoops!* I thought and laughed inside. The more I think about that blunder, however, the more I like it. I know that it should be "God the Eternal Father," but as we make God and Christ *internal* and part of us, we begin to become *eternal*. Self-worth and love cannot be separated from God. If we remove eternity from our self-concept, self-esteem becomes nothing more or less than pride and conceit. Elder Hartman Rector Jr. once said, "Self-esteem is vitally important to successful performance. Self-esteem is different than conceit—conceit is the weirdest disease in the world. It makes everyone sick except the one who has it." ("Following Christ to Victory," *Ensign,* May 1979, p. 29.) As we internalize God the Father and Jesus Christ, we begin to see as they see, love as they love, feel as they feel. Therefore, we see ourselves as they see us.

The amazing thing about an eternal perspective offered by God the Father and Jesus Christ is that their perspective allows individuals to see more in themselves than they could possibly imagine otherwise. While the price to obtain this perspective may seem more than you can afford or the climb appear more strenuous than you have strength for, the journey is worth every ounce of determination that you can muster. What does God see? "In God's eyes," Elder Marvin J. Ashton said, "nobody is a nobody. We should never lose sight of what we may become and who we are." ("While They Are Waiting," *Ensign,* May 1988, p. 63.) Brigham Young felt that "the least, the most inferior spirit now upon the earth . . . is worth worlds" (in *Journal of Discourses* 9:124).

In times of discouragement we tend to slide down the Lord's mountain and lose his perspective. We must remember Elder George Q. Cannon's comment, "We who feel ourselves sometimes so worthless, so good-for-nothing, we are not so worthless as we think. There is not one of us but what God's love has been expended upon. There is not one of us that He has not cared for and caressed. There is not one of us that He has not desired to save and that He has not devised means to save. . . . We may be insignificant and contemptible in our own eyes and in the eyes of others, but the truth remains that we are the children of God and that He has actually given His angels . . . charge concerning us, and they watch over us and have us in their keeping." (*Gospel Truth,* comp. Jerreld L. Newquist, 2 vols. [Salt Lake City: Deseret Book Co., 1974], 1:2.) It almost sounds like we can't fail, doesn't it? As we begin to understand God's grand vision for us, we understand that his standards are true and just. Rather than requiring us to measure up to others as the world's standards do, the

Lord's standards remind us that "it is not requisite that a man should run faster than he has strength" (Mosiah 4:27).

My greatest wish as a teacher and as a father is that those under my tutelage could somehow see what I see when I look into their eyes, watch them as they grow, and feel of their strong spirits. I see strong, faithful, and able young men and women who defy the world's standard and stand by their friendship with their selves. They, like my little Megan, love themselves not in any conceited or proud way but due to a combination of *internal* and *eternal.* I see such a vision in those who believe in Christ.

Jesus Christ has an uncanny way of helping others see more in themselves than they can see on their own. I remember when Christ called Peter "rock" (Matthew 16:18). I know there are significant symbolic reasons for Christ doing this, but at the same time I can't help but wonder how that made Peter feel about himself. I imagine him saying, "Did you hear that, Andrew? Rock!" Christ called James and John the "sons of thunder" (see Mark 3:17). Wow! What a nickname. I can only imagine how James and John must have felt.

I have had the opportunity on many occasions to ascend the mountain of God and see in a small way how he sees me. I have read my patriarchal blessing so many times that it is tattered and worn. I have accepted callings that I couldn't believe the Lord would extend to me. My prayers have been answered even though I still have such a long way to go. For all those times that I stood on holy ground, I found that I desired to see more of the me that God and Christ see. Their perspective is clear, far-reaching, and true. It is comforting and gives me hope.

Love as God and Christ Love

As we gain eternal perspective, we learn to love ourselves and others as God the Father and Christ love. I can only hope that you have felt that love which allows individuals to love themselves. When I was very young, I remember watching a movie called *Spartacus* about a slave who led fellow slaves against the Roman Empire. In the final battle, the Roman legions proved too strong and destroyed most of the slave army and took a large number of prisoners. Among the prisoners was Spartacus himself. The Roman leaders told the prisoners that their lives would be spared if they would identify Spartacus. Feeling that he had failed his men, that he was defeated and without comfort, Spartacus started to rise to his feet and face his fate alone. Although I was very young, what happened next made such an impression upon me that I doubt I will ever forget it. Before Spartacus could identify himself, a man chained next to him leaped to his feet and cried out, "I am Spartacus." Almost immediately, another chained prisoner arose and shouted the same confession. This continued until all the prisoners, hundreds of them, stood shouting, "I am Spartacus!" Spartacus stood silently, realizing his friends' devotion, love, and support, and wept.

I have felt that kind of friendship of love, comfort, and support before. Many times I have been accused, felt alone, or become deprived of adequate strength to stand alone. I have heard comments that destroyed my confidence, I have seen people laugh, I have felt the bite of sarcasm, and I have even been rejected by my best friends. At times like these, I have felt my heart cry out, "Is there anybody who will claim me as their friend and stand beside me? Is there anyone who loves me?" In such moments of despair, when it seems that no one else would claim me, Jesus Christ would leap to his feet and boldly answer: "I will be your friend and stand by you, for I still love you." Even when we sin or make mistakes, Christ leaps to his feet and shoulders the pain. No matter the severity of your mistake, Christ stands by you and claims you as his beloved friend. When we feel that love, we can then love ourselves and literally become our own friend. After all, the term *friend* is actually derived from the Old English *freon,* meaning "to love."

Be True, Be There

One of my favorite men from the scriptures is Joseph of Egypt. I love to read about him because of his undaunted dedication to doing what was right. I have often thought of what it would be like to have a friend like Joseph. More important, however, is the thought of what it would be like to be a friend like Joseph. His internal commitment and eternal perspective carried him through more difficult times than most of us will ever face. I am confident that the secret to Joseph's success was his friendship with God, upon which he founded a lasting friendship with himself. When faced with a dilemma of proper conduct, Joseph demonstrated his faithful commitment to his internal and eternal friendship. In a simple yet wonderfully powerful response, Joseph answered Potiphar's tempting wife by saying, "How then can I do this great wickedness, and sin against God?" (Genesis 39:9.)

Joseph's firm dedication not only to God but to himself reminds me of Bishop Robert D. Hales's comment that "a true friend will help us return with honor" ("The Aaronic Priesthood: Return with Honor," *Ensign,* May 1990, p. 40). During Joseph's crisis, he appeared to stand alone against Potiphar's wife. Yet his friend, himself, stood at his side and helped him "return with honor." Learning to stand faithful and true to yourself is highlighted by a line from Shakespeare's *Hamlet.* Polonius, an insightful counselor and friend of Hamlet, advised, "This above all: to thine own self be true" (*Hamlet,* act 1, scene 3, line 78).

I hope that when jeers, laughs, and sarcasm fill your ears; when you are scorned by your once-best friends or feel desperately alone; when your yearbook is void of signatures; when nobody is in the stands to cheer you on; when you fail an exam, aren't asked out on a date, have never been to a prom, have been involved in sins and transgressions; or when your heart desperately cries out, "Is there anybody who will claim me as their friend and stand beside me? Is there anyone that loves me?" I hope that *you* will stand up and shout, "I will stand by you. I am your friend! I still love you." If you can combine the eternal with the internal, you will *never* stand alone. You will always be cheered, encouraged, comforted, and loved when you stand true . . . to thine own self.

Matt Richardson has taught seminary and now teaches in the religion department at Brigham Young University. He speaks at many Especially for Youth, Know Your Religion, and Education Week programs. He and his wife, Lisa, are the parents of three children.

3

BEING FRIENDS WITH YOUR PARENTS

Brad Wilcox

I loved my parents until I entered seventh grade. Then I found out it wasn't cool to love your parents. I remember hearing other students talk about how mean, unfair, and old-fashioned their parents were, and I decided that if I planned to survive in this new environment, I had better start hating my parents. So I hated them. It wasn't as easy as I first thought, because I really loved them, but a man's gotta do what a man's gotta do.

All the way home on the bus, I tried to hate them. All the way up my long driveway, I told myself I hated them. I flopped down in front of the TV and reminded myself to hate them. But you just can't hate your mom and dad when you're watching *The Brady Bunch*. I decided to go outside to the field behind my house. *Outdoors is the proper place to hate parents*, I said to myself knowingly.

Between my house and the field was a barbed-wire fence. All my life I had gone under the fence, but now, being a man, I determined to go over the fence. I grabbed the top of the rough wooden fence post with my right hand and began climbing the barbed wire until I straddled the fence with one leg on each side. At that moment I thought, *This is about the dumbest thing I've ever done.* Suddenly, the barbed wire on which I was balancing gave out. I landed forcefully on the fence, and the jagged wooden post shot through my right hand—yes, in one side and out the other. Believe me, my first thought was not *I hate my parents.* I began yelling for my mom and dad as loudly as I could. I did not care if they were at the South Pole, they were going to hear me!

My dad was driving up the driveway. He heard me screaming and rushed to the fence. He pulled my hand off the post, wrapped it in a dish towel, and hurried me to the hospital emergency room. Not once did I think, *I can't stand this guy. He doesn't like my music. He doesn't like my hair.* Not once did I think, *I am going to be so embarrassed if any of my friends see me with my dad.* And I sure didn't think, *My dad is so old-fashioned to still believe in emergency rooms!* On the contrary, I felt grateful that my dad was there and was willing to help me when I got myself into such a ridiculous mess.

The entire time the doctor stitched my right hand back together, my dad sat next to me, holding my left hand and squeezing it over and over. I'll never forget the love I felt from my dad that day—the very day I had decided I was going to hate him.

President Ezra Taft Benson taught, "Your most important friendships should be with your own brothers and sisters and with your father and mother" ("To the 'Youth of the Noble Birthright,'" *Ensign,* May 1986, p. 43). That day I found out just how important parental friendships are. Happily, in all the years since that incident I have enjoyed a close friendship with my own parents and my in-laws.

As young people grow up and strive for independence, it is natural to sometimes react negatively to parents and home situations, as I did in seventh grade. Sister Virginia H. Pearce, daughter of President Gordon B. Hinckley, said: "I was in my early teens when Dad was called to be [a General Authority]. When you're in that stage of your life, your parents don't look perfect. In fact, they look less than perfect, and I was quite aware of any human foibles that my parents displayed, and so the call came as a little faith crisis for me. I thought, *How could the Lord call somebody like my dad, who is so average and sometimes lacking?*" (*Gordon B. Hinckley: Fifteenth President of the Church* [video, 1995]).

As Sister Pearce grew and matured, she came to see her father differently. She realized that the "human foibles" that seemed so obvious when she was younger were really nothing when compared with her father's goodness.

When we are young we must strive to keep the sometimes less-than-perfect actions of our parents in perspective. Are the things that bother us deliberate sins or unintentional mistakes? Might we feel differently about our parents' actions if we thought about the environments in which they grew up and the many intense pressures adults face? President Ezra Taft Benson said, "Let us also learn to be forgiving of our parents, who, perhaps having made mistakes as they reared us, almost always did the best they knew how. May we ever forgive them as we would likewise wish to be forgiven by our own children for mistakes we make." ("To the Elderly in the Church," *Ensign,* November 1989, pp. 6–7.)

Some of us hold in our minds a picture of family perfection I jokingly refer to as the "Mormon mold." The picture portrays worthy, dedicated parents surrounded by grateful, obedient children all kneeling together in family prayer. Their home swells with Church music. Each evening as they gather to enjoy their nutritious dinner, even the youngest children engage in stimulating discussions on scriptural topics. Everyone exercises daily, completes chores happily, says "I love you," and comes out of dental check-ups without a single cavity.

While such a picture is nice as an ideal, it is far from essential for our salvation or happiness. Elder Dallin H. Oaks reminded us that "today very few of our youth experience the consistent, family-centered activities of earlier times" ("Parental Leadership in the Family," *Ensign*, June 1985, p. 9). Many today grow up in nontraditional families, and we must understand that while nontraditional circumstances and relationships present some definite challenges, such individual differences do not need to hinder our personal progress.

President Howard W. Hunter has been described as nontraditional. His ancestors were not famous Church leaders. In fact, President Hunter's father was not even a member during the years when Howard was young, so he grew up in a part-member family. His mother saw to it that her two children stayed active, but when they reached age eight, their father would not give them permission for baptism. Howard was twelve and a half and his sister, Dorothy, was ten and a half before their father finally permitted them to be baptized. Howard did not serve a formal mission, and he did not attend college until after he was married in the temple and had started to raise his family. Certainly President Hunter's background was not from any predictable Mormon mold. Still, it did not keep him from progressing, being worthy, fulfilling his foreordained mission, and living a most beautiful and Christlike life. (See Eleanor Knowles, *Howard W. Hunter* [Salt Lake City: Deseret Book Co., 1994].)

It is easy to respond, "Yes, but President Hunter's parents were good people. Even though his father was not a member of the Church, he was still an honorable man. What about those who are not so fortunate?" It's true that some come from homes quite different from President Hunter's, President Hinckley's, or even my own. Some grow up in homes characterized by physical and verbal abuse and by hateful acts that leave deep wounds. How do children in such situations follow the commandment to honor their parents? (See Exodus 20:12; Mosiah 13:20.)

One girl wrote, "My father is a transvestite. He doesn't live with us anymore, but you have no idea how much what he does affects me." A young man wrote, "My dad left my mother several years ago because he chose to live a homosexual lifestyle. I fake like it doesn't bother me, but deep down it eats at me every hour

I'm awake." Another boy wrote, "My mother always abused us, not physically but mentally and emotionally. She manipulated my sisters and me and made us feel totally worthless." A young woman explained, "My father abused me sexually for years and then lied his way through every interview so he could still hold a temple recommend." How do these young people honor such dishonorable parents? The answer to such a question is often personal and never easy. It may take many years to resolve such deep hurt, anger, and frustration.

A student at Brigham Young University wanted to learn more about this topic because of struggles she had faced with her parents. She searched carefully through many Church books and magazines but found little. She said, "There's a lot of counsel on how to be a good parent and even a lot of advice on dealing with prodigal children, but very little has been written for children who have to deal with unrighteous parents." She is correct. Responding to unrighteous parents is a sensitive issue that has not been frequently addressed, perhaps because such situations and relationships are usually so complex that advice of a general nature offers little help. But if the issue is not addressed at all, those whose parents are involved in negative behavior and abuse may misunderstand the silence and suppose that no one is aware of or cares about their pain. They may mistakenly assume that they are the only ones dealing with such challenges.

The following ideas have been compiled to offer some perspective and hope—especially on down days. I realize this advice is far from complete, but regardless of the situations in our lives over which we have no control, each of us can seek to learn, to lift, and to love.

Seek to Learn

Part of my responsibilities at Brigham Young University have included supervising student teachers in their public school assignments. One young woman was extremely frustrated because the cooperating teacher to whom she had been assigned was definitely not going to be winning any teaching awards in the near future. During one of my visits, the student teacher pulled me aside to comment on dozens of things she felt the classroom teacher was doing wrong.

Admittedly, I had to cringe at some of the out-of-date practices of the cooperating teacher, but with all the professionalism I could muster I reminded the student teacher that she was a guest in that teacher's classroom and encouraged her to worry about her own performance only.

Several days later I checked back. To my surprise the student teacher seemed happier. "Has the teacher improved?" I asked her privately.

"No," she replied, "but I have discovered that I can learn just as much from a bad example as I can from a good one." Like this student teacher, those in negative situations at home can still learn positive lessons.

A boy I'll call Mike acquired this technique of learning from a bad example in his home. Mike grew up with a dictatorial father he felt he could not please. Mike was continually being compared with his brothers and coming up short. It seemed that nothing he did was good enough for his father. To make matters worse, Mike's father had a sharp temper, and any disagreement usually ended in a heavy-handed whipping.

As Mike grew up he made several promises to himself that when he had children of his own he would not repeat his father's mistakes. Mike determined that although he could not change what had happened with his father in the past, he could learn from the experiences. Coming from a dysfunctional home did not mean he had to be dysfunctional himself.

Mike served a mission, married in the temple, had children, and remained true to his private promises made as a teenager. Mike was sensitive to his children's feelings. He accepted their individual differences and did not compare them with each other. He praised positive behavior, and when a child's behavior was not so positive, he talked to that child privately rather than exploding in front of everyone as his father had done. Remembering how he craved approval and affection as a child, he hugged and kissed his own children daily and attended one child's musical concerts as often as he attended another's sports events.

Now, many years later, children and grandchildren who have been blessed by Mike's good example are thankful he learned so much from a bad one. Mike explained, "I think the essence of honoring dishonorable parents is to let any cycle of negative behavior stop with you. That's what I tried to do. It hasn't always been easy, but when I felt sorry for myself it helped to look around and see that others were also dealing with less-than-perfect family circumstances. I knew many people who were remaining active in the Church, fulfilling callings, attending to their duties, and finding a great deal of joy in their lives despite their parents' problems."

Even prophets have had to cope with unrighteous parents. Scriptures teach us that Abraham, the great and noble father of nations, had a father who was wicked, abusive, and sinful. Yes, it appears that the "grandfather" of nations is quite a blotch on the old family tree.

I cannot imagine a more difficult test for Abraham than being commanded to sacrifice his son—not only because he would lose his son, but also because Abraham knew firsthand the terror of having been part of an attempted sacrifice at the hands of his own father (see Abraham 1:7–17,30). Could we tell Abraham anything he does not already know about recurring nightmares, private tears, and seemingly uncontrollable anger that results when someone in a position of authority and trust exercises unrighteous dominion?

No one in dysfunctional family circumstances would ever wish the same on another soul. Still, there can be great comfort in knowing that others who have had to deal with similar trials have survived. As we seek to learn, we can draw strength and courage from their experiences.

Seek to Lift

President Harold B. Lee said, "You cannot lift another soul until you are standing on higher ground than he is. You must be sure, if you would rescue the man, that you yourself are setting the example of what you would have him be." (*Stand Ye in Holy Places* [Salt Lake City: Deseret Book Co., 1974], p. 187.)

One student at BYU asserted, "The idea is not to get a chalkboard and teach gospel lessons out of a manual. The idea is to quietly be the best example you can." She is correct. President David O. McKay told us, "The most effective way to teach religion in the home is not by preaching but by living" (in Conference Report, April 1955, p. 27).

While we will not be held accountable for the salvation of others—even our parents—we will be held accountable for our actions and for the way we let our own lights shine. President Spencer W. Kimball advised that one of the best ways to honor our parents is by our own righteous living (see *The Teachings of Spencer W. Kimball* [Salt Lake City: Bookcraft, 1982], p. 348).

"But what if your parents don't want your good example and righteous living?" wrote one girl, JoAnn. "The rules in my house were *don't* go to Church and *do* smoke, drink, yell, and swear. The reward I received for being an example was for my parents to kick me out and disown me."

I'm afraid there are too many who can relate to JoAnn's words. My wife and I have a dear friend in Texas who joined the Church despite her parents' strong disapproval. She did not want to hurt her mother and father by going against their wishes, but she knew that, as President Benson said, "Sometimes one must choose to honor a Heavenly Father over a mortal father" (*The Teachings of Ezra Taft Benson* [Salt Lake City: Bookcraft, 1988],

p. 350). Her parents had warned her she would be disowned if she joined the Church, and on the day of her baptism they made good the threat. It was difficult, but our friend remained true to her covenants.

She soon met a wonderful returned missionary and became engaged even though her parents were horrified to think she would be married in a Mormon temple. Not only did her parents choose not to attend, they sent letters to all friends and relatives who had been invited to the reception telling them not to attend or send gifts.

Such behavior hurt the newlywed couple deeply. They felt like saying, "Well, if that's the way you're going to be, then fine. If you don't want anything to do with us, we don't want anything to do with you either." But this couple knew that however natural the tendency to return hate for hate and however justified we may sometimes feel in seeking revenge, these efforts are ultimately wasted. Elder Richard G. Scott said, "Bitterness and hatred are harmful. They produce much that is destructive. They postpone the relief and healing you yearn for." ("Healing the Tragic Scars of Abuse," *Ensign,* May 1992, p. 33.)

The young couple knew that if they truly wanted to lift their parents, they would have to stay on higher ground regardless of the pain, unfairness, and hurt involved. President Gordon B. Hinckley affirmed, "Let us reach out with love and kindness to those who would revile against us. . . . In the spirit of the Christ who advised us to turn the other cheek, let us try to overcome evil with good." ("Reach Out in Love and Kindness," *Ensign,* November 1982, p. 77.)

Happily, this wonderful couple decided, "Our parents may shut us out of their lives right now, but we will not shut them out of ours." Each Sunday evening they phoned her parents, just as they phoned his parents.

Another blow came when the young couple announced their first baby. Her parents said that since they did not acknowledge her wedding because it had been performed in a Mormon temple, in their eyes this baby was illegitimate. Still the couple continued to be true to the Church and stay on higher ground. This couple is letting their light shine, and although her parents don't want to see it right now, the example these two are offering could one day save her parents.

In the Book of Mormon we read about Joseph of old, who was "preserved by the hand of the Lord, that he might preserve his father, Jacob, and all his household from perishing with famine" (1 Nephi 5:14). I think the same could be said of our friend from Texas—she has been preserved by the hand of the Lord that perhaps one day she might preserve her father and family from perishing with spiritual famine.

It's not always easy to stay on higher ground. Joseph Smith and Jesus Christ both faced authorities who ridiculed, critics who hounded, and mobs who mercilessly persecuted. Still, rather than lowering themselves to the level of their tormenters, they remained on higher ground and lifted others. Another one of my heroes is the great educator Booker T. Washington. An African-American born into slavery, he lived through a time of intense prejudice and hatred. Yet he lived by this rule: "I shall allow no man to belittle my soul by making me hate him" (in *A New Treasury of Words to Live By,* sel. William Nichols [New York: Simon and Schuster, 1947], p. 132).

President Benson once asked, "Children, do you pray for your parents? . . . They, like you, will make mistakes but they have a divine mission to accomplish in your life. Will you help them do so?" He also spoke to parents about their children, but the counsel would be applicable even if the roles were reversed: "And if your [parent] went temporarily astray, do you think it would please the Lord and He would honor your efforts if you continued to live an exemplary life, consistently prayed and frequently fasted for that [parent], and kept the name of that [father] or [mother] on the temple prayer roll?" (*The Teachings of Ezra Taft Benson,* p. 351.)

A young convert I shall call Don was in a home situation

where conversations consisted mostly of put-downs, dirty jokes, swear words, and less-than-subtle innuendoes. Don realized the atmosphere was polluting him in ways that were affecting his spirituality. When he heard himself start to laugh at the jokes and join in the put-downs, he decided to make a change—not in his living arrangements, but in his attitude. He knew he had little control over the language of his parents and siblings, but he could control whether he would join them. Elder Richard G. Scott said, "The wicked choice of others cannot completely destroy your agency unless you permit it" ("Healing," p. 31).

Seek to Love

Elder F. Enzio Busche said, "We, in our imperfect bodies and in our strivings for perfection, are confronted with situations where members of our own families . . . can behave like an enemy. Then the time comes when love as a power is needed and tested, for the person who has earned love the least needs it the most." ("Love Is the Power That Will Cure the Family," *Ensign*, May 1982, p. 70.)

A young man from Nevada had a rough stepfather who was disappointed in his stepson because of the boy's interest in religion. This stepfather saw faith as a weakness and was actually upset that this teenager wouldn't prove his manhood by fighting, drinking, and chasing girls. When the boy was eighteen, he was introduced to the LDS church and joined. Soon after his baptism, his stepfather kicked him out. The young man was invited to move in with a Latter-day Saint family in his ward as he worked and prepared for his mission.

When he entered the Missionary Training Center, he wrote a letter: "We heard a talk in which we were told to express our love to our parents. I wondered how I would ever be able to love my stepfather when I don't even like him very much. Then I realized that loving someone doesn't mean I have to spend a lot of time with him, emulate him, or follow him in unrighteousness. For me right now, loving him means that I feel sorry for him and that I won't give up hope that one day he might change."

Another part of love is forgiveness. One young woman approached her leader at a summer youth program at BYU, confused about her relationship with her parents. She said, "I know the scriptures say you must forgive everyone, but my parents don't deserve forgiveness after all they have done." The leader suggested that even if her parents did not merit forgiveness, she still needed to forgive them—if not for their sakes then for her own. Elder Scott said, "Forgiveness heals terrible, tragic wounds, for it allows the love of God to purge your heart and mind of the poison of hate. It cleanses your consciousness of the desire for revenge. It makes place for the purifying, healing, restoring love of the Lord." ("Healing," p. 33.)

Later this young lady wrote her leader a letter. "I thought about what you said for a long time, and I decided you were right—I didn't want you to be, but you are. I am not the judge— God is. I will leave it in his hands." Years later, as a college student, this young woman shared even more of her experience. She wrote, "Deciding to forgive my parents and actually doing it were two different stories. I understood the principle involved, but I had a hard time implementing it because of all I had suffered—not just the physical pain but the emotional losses. Every morning I would pray to Heavenly Father to help me forgive and let go of my ill feelings toward them. Every night I would still be filled with bitterness and even occasionally dream of seeking revenge and getting even."

The young woman explained how this went on for several years. She said, "Then I felt the Spirit leave me. That was the start of an ordeal I never want to repeat, but in an effort to regain the blessings of the Spirit in my own life, I finally let forgiveness and love for my parents enter my heart." She had no intention of reestablishing ties or inviting their involvement in her decisions; to do so while they remained unrepentant would have only opened the door for further abuse, manipulation, and problems. Forgiveness did not require that this young woman rekindle relationships with dangerous people. It simply meant that she was finally able to let go of her resentment and anger.

Seeking to learn, to lift, and to love may not be a complete solution to every problem, but it is a perspective with which to begin. Further help is available through priesthood leaders and sometimes through professional sources they may recommend. Most important, the best help is always available from our Father in Heaven—a perfect parent worthy of all honor and praise. As we pray and ask Heavenly Father for assistance, we can trust he will lead us (see James 1:5–6; Moroni 7:26). We will not be left comfortless (see John 14:18).

Sister Joy F. Evans told of a father who took his young children to a lake for their vacation. He taught his nine-year-old how to manage a small sailboat and then, fastening him in a life jacket, he let the boy take the boat out onto the lake by himself. After a while, the father felt he should make sure all was well, so in another little boat he sailed out to his son. When the father arrived, the boy was sitting calmly in the boat. He had forgotten how to turn it around, but he wasn't worried. He looked up at his dad and said, "I knew you'd come." (See "Overcoming Challenges Along Life's Way," *Ensign,* November 1987, p. 92.) In the same way, when we feel lost and sometimes wonder what to do, we can feel confident that our Heavenly Father will come to our aid.

Brad Wilcox *is on the faculty of the elementary education department at Brigham Young University. He is the author of several books and talk tapes and speaks frequently at Especially for Youth and Education Week programs. He and his wife, Deborah Gunnell Wilcox, have four children.*

4

BEING FRIENDS WITH YOUR BROTHERS AND SISTERS

John Bytheway

A long time ago, you signed up to be on a team. You may not remember signing up—in fact, none of us do. But you're on a team, and you're contributing to it right now, as we speak. Look down at your feet. Are they moving? Yes, they are. I mean, I hope they are; otherwise, you're just coasting and not contributing.

The Tour de Family

You see, when a couple gets married, it's as if they climb onto a tandem bike, or a "bicycle built for two." A tandem bike has two sets of pedals, two sets of handlebars, and two seats. The couple leave the wedding reception and pedal off together, both moving in the same direction. They get used to each other. They notice how each partner handles the turns and reacts to other hazards in the road. They make adjustments for one another. They pedal up hills and through valleys. It's the beginning of a great team.

After a while, they decide it might be nice to have someone else to ride with them, and they begin having children. When the first arrival comes, they install another seat, another set of handlebars, and two more pedals. They know this new addition to the team won't be able to pedal for a while, but the pedals are there and can be used as soon as those little feet can reach down and touch them. For now, the parents take responsibility for the extra weight of the new teammate and keep pedaling as they have done before. Soon they add another teammate and another, both parents looking over their shoulders with joy at these new young cyclists. The bike is a little heavier now and a little longer. It takes a little more coordination to get around the turns and negotiate the chuckholes. But Father is strong, and Mother is wise, and the *Tour de Family* keeps cruisin' down the road.

Then one day something wonderful happens. The first child reaches down with his or her feet and starts to pedal. Father looks back with a grin, Mother is smiling, and the other siblings are laughing with glee. This is fun! The other siblings watch wide-eyed as the oldest pedals along. *Just like Mom and Dad!* they say to themselves. *I'm gonna pedal just like that someday.* Another teammate is added, and then perhaps another. Soon the team is complete, and our cyclist heroes—Mom, Dad, and children—cruise smoothly down the road. There are rough roads ahead. There is bad weather, chuckholes, and fog. But the team is prepared, they know what lies ahead, and the *Tour de Family* glides on by.

Where are they going? Is it a real race? Who wins? Well, the *Tour de Family* is different from most races. You're not racing against any other families. You're just trying to do the best you can with the team you're on, endure to the end, and cross the final finish line with no empty seats. Each family has a different road. We cannot control what road we are given; we can only react to it. Some teams are captained by mothers alone. They pedal very hard and are sometimes very weary. This is when good teammates must dig in and pedal with all their might to help Mom.

We've all seen teams in the *Tour de Family* that make us sad. Some sons or daughters refuse to pedal and instead just coast. Some siblings even put on the brakes, slowing the family on its course and making the other teammates work even harder.

On some teams, one very strong sibling can make a tremendous difference for good. On one family team there was a very strong young man named Nephi. He pedaled as hard as he could, all the time. Wherever Father Lehi steered the family, Nephi was willing to follow. Nephi had brothers who seemed to put on the brakes now and then. They made Lehi and Sariah very weary. There was another brother named Sam who watched Nephi and, to the benefit of the team, followed what Nephi did. And there were times when Nephi moved the entire bicycle all by himself!

You, young reader, are old enough to put your feet down and pedal too. You know it because most of you have been out there already, pedaling for a long time. Some of you started pedaling before you could read! Behind you and perhaps in front of you, other siblings are contributing too.

As a teammate you can do one of three things: you can pedal, you can coast, or you can put on the brakes. Applying the hand brake while others are trying to pedal is considered rude. Coasting or acting like you're pedaling is not as bad, but it makes the others work harder. The most important thing to remember is that *whatever you do, it affects the whole team.*

How can you be a friend to your siblings? How can you affect your team for good? There must be a million ways. We'll talk about a few. But first, let's talk about the word *friend*. My favorite definition comes from Elder Robert D. Hales of the Quorum of the Twelve Apostles: "A true friend makes it easier for us to live the gospel by being around him" ("The Aaronic Priesthood: Return with Honor," *Ensign,* May 1990, p. 40). That is a wonderful definition. Do you make it easier for your brothers and sisters to live the gospel? If so then you are a friend of the very best kind. I would like to talk about three ways we can be a friend to our siblings: We can be a good example, we can concentrate on giving instead of receiving, and we can always choose to love.

Being an Example

In my *Tour de Family*, I was in seat number seven. My oldest brother David sat in seat number three, right behind Mom. I remember looking ahead at one point on our bicycle built for eight and David was gone. What happened? David had gone to Arizona to serve a mission. He was off riding another kind of tandem bike with what they call a "companion." We would miss his strong legs, but every time we received a letter from David, we all got very excited and pedaled even harder. Can you imagine what it did to the rest of us as we watched our oldest brother leave and go on a mission? He set a precedent for all the boys on the team. Somewhere inside I said, *I'm gonna do that one day.* It wasn't many years later that the number six spot became vacant: my other brother Kendrick was off on a mission to Japan. He must have said the same thing to himself that I did when we saw David leave. Both of my brothers are true friends to all their siblings. By setting an example, they made it easier for me to live the gospel of Jesus Christ. Soon my turn came, and I served a mission in the Philippines.

Can you imagine what you can do for your family? There must be a million ways you can set an example. You can laugh while you do your chores, you can stop quarrels before they start, and you can help with the housework. You can pray! I have always been touched by a certain passage in the Book of Mormon: "And no tongue can speak, neither can there be written by any man, neither can the hearts of men conceive so great and marvelous things as we both saw and heard Jesus speak; and no one can conceive of the joy which filled our souls at the time we heard him pray for us unto the Father" (3 Nephi 17:17).

Can you imagine hearing Jesus himself pray for you? What would that have been like? Jesus is the Son of God and our Savior. We can also say that Jesus is our friend in the very best sense of the word, because his example makes it easier for us to live the gospel. How can we follow him? We follow him by doing what he did. Imagine the power you can have in your own family if, when you offer the family prayer, you mention your parents and each of your brothers and sisters by name and lovingly pray for them! If there isn't regular family prayer in your home, imagine the power you can have to bless your family if *you* organize it! You can be a Nephi and take charge, pedaling the whole family if needed. Be a friend to your siblings by setting an example every day.

Giving Instead of Receiving

Being a good teammate comes from having a good attitude. We need to ask ourselves some important questions: Am I going to help this family make progress, or am I going to put on the brakes and make them carry me along? Will I continually point out what is wrong in our family, or will I work to make things right? Will I be a part of the solution or a part of the problem? Family life is wonderful, but we all know it's not always easy. Every teammate brings his or her own personality and preferences. The family is a workshop to help you confront and conquer your own weaknesses.

Have you ever wanted to stand up during family home evening and say, "When are you people going to completely devote yourselves to making me happy?" If you adopt that attitude, be prepared for disappointment. In being a friend to your siblings, you will succeed if you always look for chances to give, not take. In the *Tour de Family*, you will succeed if you always look for chances to pedal, not coast.

I had a chance to make a difference in my family a few years ago. I think that's why I was asked to write this chapter. One December night at a family Christmas party, my oldest brother, David, asked if he could talk to me. We went into the front room, where he told me that he was sick again. This wasn't just any kind of sick. This was big-time, "I'm going to die if something doesn't change" type of sick. David continued, "It looks like I'm going to need one of your kidneys." Fortunately, all of us are born with a spare kidney. We don't have a spare heart or brain, but we do have a spare kidney. In fact, the body uses only about half of one kidney at any given moment.

Eight years earlier, we had gone to the hospital to prepare for a transplant surgery. They tested everyone in the family to see who had the best match. It was me. But there was a problem: I had just received my mission call. I was to report to the missionary training center within two months. We didn't know what to do. We asked our stake president, and he called the missionary committee of the Church. The problem was explained to Elder Bruce R. McConkie. He considered the situation and finally said, "Send the boy on a mission." So I went. About a month later, I received a letter from David that said, "Hey, everything seems to be okay. My kidneys are fine for now. Have a great mission!" And I did. I learned once again that God knows what he's doing and that he is a god of miracles.

Now, years later, David was sick again. I had a chance to do something for my brother that no one else could do. I had a chance to give, not take. I was honored to do it. I was proud that I had a drug-free, alcohol-free, tobacco-free kidney. When the transplant coordinator came into the hospital room to speak to us, she looked at David and asked, "Are you the recipient?" David said yes. She looked at me and asked, "Are you the donor?" I said yes. She looked at David and said, "In a couple of days, you're going to feel great." Then she looked at me and said,

"You will be in a significant amount of pain." I thought to myself, "Boy, she doesn't beat around the bush." After that, she showed a video called, "So, You're Having an Operation." This video was without question one of the grossest things I had ever seen in my life. Don't rent it! After the video, David and I exchanged glances. We both had that "Gee, this is gonna be fun" look on our faces.

After chatting with the doctors and a man from the National Kidney Foundation, I was given a bottle of special soap and told to get up early and shower. Then I was to put on some special clothes and sit on my bed for someone to come get me (believe me, I wasn't going anywhere wearing those "special clothes"). They took me at about 7:00 A.M., and I awoke in my room at about 2:30 in the afternoon. My mom was standing at the foot of the bed, and my dad was in fetal position on the floor. This seemed a little odd. Apparently I had been moaning in pain for the past few hours, and my dad could hardly stand it, so he curled up on the floor. I remember asking Mom how David was doing, and then I felt the "significant pain." Oh, yes. It was definitely pain, and it was significant. Ouch-o-rama!

I looked around the room and saw other members of my family. All were smiling but close to tears. It was a very amazing day. The love and concern and feeling of family were so thick in that room you could cut it with a knife (oooh, bad choice of words). The next day, when I saw David, was one of the best days of my life. He looked so good. (He still does.) I've wondered on occasion why the Lord just didn't heal David when I went on my mission. I know he could have, but I'm glad he didn't because I learned a powerful lesson that I'm making a feeble attempt to share with you now. The last five paragraphs were written to prepare you for this one sentence. Are you ready? Here it comes: If you want to be happy in your family, always look for chances to give, not take. Always look for chances to pedal, not coast. There are some steep hills ahead. You are part of the team! They need you! You need them! The *Tour de Family* needs to cross the finish line with no empty seats. So, to alter an old phrase, "Ask not what your family can do for you, but what you can do for your family." If I could bring my family that close together again, I'd consider giving up another major body part.

Choose to Love

As human beings, we can choose how we're going to act and react. This makes life fun, because it means we can do things that are totally unexpected. One day I went into the bathroom and started turning everything of my sister's upside down. Every bottle, jar, or can of stuff that I could find I turned upside down. Shampoo, antiperspirant, makeup, hair spray, cologne—you name it, I inverted it. It looked pretty funny. I put an ugly, plastic toy frog next to the upside-down items to make it look like the frog did it. I don't remember why I did all this, but I know it was unexpected. The next time my sister Jeri walked into the bathroom, I heard a "What in the wo—" followed by laughter. I could hear her laughing, and I was silently laughing nearby. For the next few months, Kendrick and Jeri and I played little harmless tricks on each other. And everytime we did something, we'd put that ugly frog toy nearby. Anytime anything strange or unexpected happened in the house, there was that mysterious frog. Years later we still laugh about those tricks and that frog.

You want to have some fun in your family? Do something unexpected. You want to create some love in your family? Do something unexplainable. I saw a bumper sticker the other day that said, "Commit random acts of kindness." Great idea! If you do one random act of service a day, in one week it will change your family, guaranteed. Try it! Next time you see some dirty dishes, do 'em! Next time you see a messy room, clean it—a dirty carpet, vacuum it! One random act a day, that's all we ask. Do it in secret, and don't explain it. And for added fun, leave an ugly frog toy nearby. This kind of "service virus" is contagious.

Your siblings will catch on. Soon all kinds of mindless acts of kindness will be happening all over the house. Mass hysteria!

The youth I admire most in the world are those who take responsibility for things that aren't their responsibility. Why be normal? Choose to be the kind of sibling you'd like to have, and it will change your family. Even if it doesn't, do it anyway! You will find as you grow older that the only person who can make you happy is you. It's also true that the only person who can make you mad is you. Being happy or sad is a decision that you make every day. Saying "She made me mad" is a falsehood. Saying "He makes me angry" is also a lie. No one can make you feel anything. You are the final decision-maker. The buck stops on your desk. You can be as happy as you decide to be. You can't spend your whole life blaming your moods and your problems on others.

Sure, there are sibling rivalries, but we have models to follow in these cases as well. You can learn how to be a family from the television or from the scriptures. If you take your lessons from the Simpsons, for example, then family life will be one smart-aleck put-down after another. If you learn from the Joseph Smith family, you'll see siblings willing to die for one another. In the words of Elder Neal A. Maxwell of the Quorum of the Twelve Apostles: "One cannot help but be struck by the nobility of a man like Hyrum Smith, an older brother, who made room for a younger brother, Joseph Smith. Hyrum gladly supported his younger brother in the marvelous things Joseph had to do, glorying in the younger brother's achievements and sharing, finally, even martyrdom as a brother." (*That My Family Should Partake* [Salt Lake City: Deseret Book Co., 1974], pp. 91–92.)

To say that Joseph and Hyrum were friends would be the understatement of the year. The scriptures tell us that "in life they were not divided, and in death they were not separated!" (D&C 135:3.) Let us use Joseph and Hyrum as a model of how to be a friend to our siblings.

Fasten Your Helmet

When I was growing up, we had quarreling in our house and we had arguments, but we did the best we knew how. If I could go back and start over, I would be different. I would be a peacemaker. I would walk away from quarrels. I would commit random acts of kindness (and I'd still leave an ugly frog toy nearby). I would help my parents move the family by pedaling a little harder, being a little nicer, and realizing that part of the responsibility of making this family work was mine. It took me a long time to realize that. I thought it was Dad's job to bring home cash, Mom's job to make it into food, and my job to eat the food and keep the hamper full of soiled clothes so Mom could wash and fold them and return them to my drawer. How selfish I was!

In our hearts, each of us knows countless ways we can be a better friend to our siblings. We don't really need this chapter, except perhaps as a reminder. The *Tour de Family* is fun! But in these last days, it's also getting more and more dangerous. There are forces who want to tear the family apart. There are rough roads ahead! It's time to fasten our helmets and strap our feet into the pedals. What a blessing you can be to your parents and your siblings if you decide to be!

May you be a valiant teammate in your *Tour de Family;* may you always be a true friend, helping your siblings to live the gospel of Jesus Christ by your example, by concentrating on pedaling instead of coasting, and by choosing to love. And may your team arrive safely across the finish line, pure and fresh and sinless, with no empty seats!

John Bytheway *is an administrator in Continuing Education at Brigham Young University. A few months after writing this chapter, he climbed onto a tandem bike with his new bride, Kimberly Ann Loveridge, and they're now pedaling happily ever after in their own* Tour de Family.

5

BEING FRIENDS WITH PEERS AT SCHOOL

Randall C. Bird

One evening my family watched the video *Charlotte's Web* together. Suprisingly, tears filled the eyes of most of us at the video's conclusion. Normally we save our tears for movies such as *Bambi* or *Old Yeller,* but this video captured our hearts and emotions.

There's a beautiful moral to this story of Charlotte and Wilbur, who are the two main characters. Charlotte, as you may recall, was a spider, while Wilbur was a pig. Wilbur had some very hard times and often felt alone and discouraged, especially when he realized that soon he would be butchered. With this sad thought on his mind and a cloudy, rainy day to match, Wilbur cried, "I need a friend!" and threw himself down in the manure and sobbed. Well, eventually Wilbur was saved by Charlotte, who ingeniously weaved messages into her web that said he was not an ordinary pig. Even Wilbur began to believe he was something special—because Charlotte told him so. Wilbur became a most famous pig, and people traveled some distance to see and honor him. Near the end of the story, Wilbur learned that a spider's life is brief and that the time was fast approaching that Charlotte would not be around to comfort him. Her life was spent preparing Wilbur for the future so that he would look for the good things in life and not be depressed and lonely. Some of her last words to her friend Wilbur, as recorded in the book version, were: "Winter will pass, the days will lengthen, the ice will melt in the pasture pond. The song sparrow will return and sing, the frogs will awake, the warm wind will blow again. All these sights and sounds and smells will be yours to enjoy, Wilbur— this lovely world, these precious days . . ."

The book continues:

> Charlotte stopped. A moment later a tear came to Wilbur's eye. "Oh, Charlotte," he said. "To think that when I first met you I thought you were cruel and bloodthirsty!"
>
> When he recovered from his emotion, he spoke again.
>
> "Why did you do all this for me?" he asked. "I don't deserve it. I've never done anything for you."
>
> "You have been my friend," replied Charlotte. "That in itself is a tremendous thing. I wove my webs for you because I liked you. After all, what's a life, anyway? We're born, we live a little while, we die. . . . By helping you, perhaps I was trying to lift up my life a trifle. Heaven knows anyone's life can stand a little of that."
>
> "Well," said Wilbur. "I'm no good at making speeches. . . . But you have saved me, Charlotte, and I would gladly give my life for you." (E. B. White, *Charlotte's Web* [New York: HarperCollins, 1952], p. 164.)

Friends can truly save each other from problems big and small. Before adulthood, most of our experiences with friendship happen at or through school. Shortly after we moved to Utah, for example, I noticed that my junior-high-aged daughter was having great fears as her first day of school approached. Many concerns occupied her mind. Who would be her friends? How would she do at a new school? And of course the big question, Who would she sit by during lunch? She had the great fear that by ninth grade everyone would have their group of friends, leaving no space for a move-in and thus leaving her all alone in some corner holding her lunch tray. She prayed daily for two weeks prior to school starting that someone would ask her to eat lunch with them.

Well, the first day of school arrived and she left for the unexpected. How grateful she was when a girl seated behind her in one of her morning classes tapped her on the shoulder and said, "Hey, would you like to eat lunch with me and my friends?" She came home from that first day of school excited and relieved and with a stronger testimony of the power of prayer. This group of girls had helped her belong. She was now a part of that school and had some friends to associate with.

The sad thing is that not all people have that good of an experience in their lives. There are those who attend schools where thousands of youth walk by them daily, and yet they feel all alone. I'm reminded of a young man who, as he was growing up, developed differently than most other boys. His physique was abnormal. His breastbone didn't sink in like most people's; instead, it poked out, giving the appearance of a chicken breast. Since he looked that way, many called him "chicken breast." He hurt each time someone referred to him that way.

On one occasion while he was eating his lunch at school, a bigger, stronger boy walked by him and called him that name. The young man stood and said, "Please don't call me that." The other boy replied, "Oh, and what are you going to do about it?" The two began to push each other back and forth until the bigger boy dropped the other boy to the floor with a blow to the head. Most of the onlookers failed to help the downed boy, but one good Samaritan stayed behind to help him. He drove the boy to his home, where his family attended to his injuries. You see, not only did this young man feel like he didn't belong, but others went to great lengths to ensure that he didn't.

This story ends on a sad note. The young man, who had been ridiculed during most of his life, finally made a decision to leave life early. He ended his life one day while the rest of his family was at church. One seriously wonders if the story could have ended on a more positive note had others been willing to help him belong and be his friend.

So how do we go about making friends at our schools? A seminary student gave the following thought one day during his devotional. He stood and jokingly said, "To have a friend is to be one." Everyone laughed and poked fun at the person who gave the thought. I sat and pondered what he'd just said. You know, how true that statement is in our schools. As we go out of our way to serve others, it seems that others care more about us, not unlike the story of Charlotte serving Wilbur.

A few years ago I was invited to speak at a youth conference in Texas. It didn't take long to see that these youth liked one another. Laughter, tears, and a good spirit permeated their meetings. During the conference I had occasion to talk to many of the participants. I found it interesting that several of them were not members of the church. I asked them why they were in attendance. Each nonmember I visited with gave the same girl's name as the reason why he or she was in attendance. Each then began to rehearse the many acts of kindness this girl had done for him or her. I was definitely anxious to meet this girl.

At the testimony meeting that concluded the conference, when a certain young woman stood to bear her testimony and tell us her name, I instantly recognized her as the girl who had befriended so many. Her testimony was pure and simple, yet it touched all in attendance. She even mentioned her friends and told them how the gospel had changed her life.

This young woman was truly practicing what the scriptures say: "And if it so be that you should labor all your days in crying repentance unto this people, and bring, save it be one soul unto me, how great shall be your joy with him in the kingdom of my Father!" (D&C 18:15.) This verse of scripture was spoken by one who, like Charlotte, stepped forth and said, "I'll be your friend." However, this friend of ours saved us from a fate much worse than being butchered; he "suffered the pain of all men, that all men might repent and come unto him" (D&C 18:11). Our Heavenly Father sees infinite worth in each of us and loved us enough to allow his Son to be sacrificed that we might live. Now he asks us to be Charlottes and help the Wilburs of the world.

The young lady at the Texas youth conference had found that to have a friend is to be one. We can do the same on a daily basis in our schools, for there are many who often have Wilbur kinds of days. We need to weave the web of kindness by helping others see those who struggle for what they really are.

Our schools usually give us a chance to see a large number of classmates each day. Learn their names! There's a certain feeling that accompanies hearing your own name. I love how the Prophet Joseph described the First Vision. He said: "When the light rested upon me I saw two Personages, whose brightness and glory defy all description, standing above me in the air. One of them spake unto me, calling me by name and said, pointing to the other—*This is My Beloved Son. Hear Him!*" (Joseph Smith—History 1:17.)

The Lord knows us by name. He calls us by name. Each day at school, learn a new name or two. Then, the next day, greet that person by using his or her name. We like to hear our names. When I was a teacher, that was one of the first things I tried to do: learn the names of my students. I didn't want to just say "Hello," I wanted to say "Hello, Julie." Recently, the Primary organization encouraged us to call the children in our wards and branches by name. Children respond warmly upon hearing their name.

Schools also provide an excellent opportunity for us to make friends through extracurricular activities as well as classroom experiences. When I taught a workshop at an Idaho State Student Council convention, many student leaders desired to learn ways they could help more students feel a part of their schools. What could student leaders do to help facilitate that experience? Activities, clubs, organizations, service groups, sports, bands, drama, homecoming, choirs, and tutoring are just a few of the experiences students could have at school that would give them an opportunity to meet and know others. I've also attended schools where assemblies honored not only the athletes but those involved in other areas of service to the school. One young lady received a standing ovation when it was announced that each week for the past four years she had donated eight hours to those with special needs at a nearby hospital. Truly, "when ye are in the service of your fellow beings ye are only in the service of your God" (Mosiah 2:17).

There's something nice about a person with a genuine smile. They make you feel good, and if you stay around them for a period of time you will probably find yourself smiling too. After graduating from high school, I attended Ricks College. I can still remember my first few days of walking across campus. I was anxious to meet and make new friends, but I had a certain shyness about approaching people. I would see a person at a distance and think, "I am going to say hello to that person." Well, as they approached, I did like many of you do: the closer they got, the more nervous I became. Just as soon as we came within good eye and voice contact, I would stare at the ground and walk on by. Then, mad at myself, I would turn around and look back towards the person I had just passed. I often wondered what would happen if they too turned around at that same moment. Would we both be in shock and quickly return to our former positions, or would we be courageous enough to say "Hi"? Well, fortunately for me, many students I passed on campus smiled and said "Hello." Can you imagine how that made me feel? I found myself eventually doing the same. Students often referred to the "spirit of Ricks." It was people being kind, considerate, and thoughtful of others that brought out this good spirit.

I remember well a young lady from a seminary class who approached me and asked, "Who can I make happier today? Have you seen anyone who needs a lift?" I thought for a few minutes, then I gave her the name of a young man who could use some cheering up. Well, I didn't need to say another word. For a solid week this young lady put nice notes, candy, and other "warm fuzzies" into this young man's locker. He didn't know who was being so kind to him; he only knew that he could hardly wait to visit his locker each day. He became a new person. He was happy about school, life, and his family. He talked more to others, and his confidence began to "wax strong" (D&C 121:45) because a girl's kindness led his thoughts toward the good things of life instead of gloom and darkness.

We enjoy being around those who make us feel better. Have you ever asked a person how he or she was doing and suddenly found yourself hearing about that person's worst day ever or his or her troubles, nightmares, and gloom? Or the person tells you everything that is wrong with everyone and everything. In such an encounter, you will probably find yourself feeling a little down. We usually don't like to be around such a person. Though we all have bad days, it's important that we rise above them. It's so enjoyable to be around someone who makes us feel better. It's been said that a person who leads you closer to God is your friend. Remember the two who traveled with Jesus following his resurrection and said, "Did not our heart burn within us, while he talked with us by the way, and while he opened to us the scriptures?" (Luke 24:32.) We should leave those we come in contact with feeling good about life.

There seems to be a misunderstanding by some people today about what it means to be a friend. Acts of a friend should result in self-improvement, better attitudes, self-reliance, comfort, consolation, self-respect, and better welfare. Certainly the word *friend* is misused if used to describe a person who contributes to our delinquency, misery, and heartaches. When we make a person feel he or she is wanted, that person's whole attitude changes. Our friendship will be recognizable if our actions and attitudes result in improvement and independence.

Quite a few years ago I was on a youth outing in Idaho at a swimming resort called Lava Hot Springs. While I was lazily enjoying myself by floating on an air mattress in the pool, a group of young women surrounded me and gave me this challenge: "Brother Bird, go dive off the high dive." As I looked up more than thirty feet in the air, the high dive seemed more like a device of torture than something fun. Who in their right mind would ever dive off such an edifice? This structure seemed it would be the vehicle of death for anyone who would attempt to dive from its platform.

Somehow, at the urging of these young women, I found myself leaving the pool and climbing the ladder toward the platform. Why was I doing such a crazy thing? Those girls, supposedly my friends, were now watching anxiously as I inched my way toward the top. Part way up, I decided to go back down. However, a young woman was on the step below me, and I couldn't let this girl know that a man had chickened out and not finished the dive. I reached the top only to see what appeared to be very small people floating in the water below. I offered to let the young girl behind me jump first, and that's exactly what she did. She left the platform feet first, entered the water, and lived through the experience. This gave me renewed hope—but I was supposed to *dive*.

I walked toward the edge of the platform and pointed my hands downward. Straight down toward the water I flew, not knowing that at such heights you should dive more out from the platform than straight down. Needless to say, about half the way down my body started to turn so that I was lying parallel to the water below. If I were to hit the water in this position, death would be a certain possibility for me.

Through no skill of my own, my body continued to turn until I had completed a full somersault, which allowed me to enter the water feet first. As I regained the surface, all of the girls were very excited. They surrounded me and screamed, "Yeah, Brother Bird, do it again!" Were these my friends? Remember, true friends give comfort and consolation and improve your happiness, leaving you better off than they found you. Our happiness certainly shouldn't depend on making someone else, even our friends, miserable.

As individuals and especially teenagers, what kinds of friends do we select, adopt, confide in, and visit with? Are we strong enough to refuse to be a friend of the world and its representatives? Are we strong enough to accept friendship with Christ? Does being a friend mean becoming complacent and surrendering to lower standards, or does it mean maintaining Christlike standards and defending them? Do we consider mutual friendship as a way to develop and maintain the foundation of our testimony of Christ? The scriptures tell us to "feast upon the words of Christ; for behold, the words of Christ will tell you all things what ye should do" (2 Nephi 32:3). The conditions are set; the model is given. Then why not become his disciple by being his witness? Why entertain a constant dilemma in your mind? Commit yourself to be his friend!

At times like today, we all need a friend, someone who will tell us how special we are, someone who will remind us of what President George Q. Cannon told us:

"Now, this is the truth. We humble people, we who feel ourselves sometimes so worthless, so good-for-nothing, we are not so worthless as we think. There is not one of us but what God's love has been expended upon. There is not one of us that He has not cared for and caressed. There is not one of us that He has not desired to save and that He has not devised means to save. There is not one of us that He has not given His angels charge concerning. We may be insignificant and contemptible in our own eyes and in the eyes of others, but the truth remains that we are the children of God and that He has actually given His angels—invisible beings of power and might—charge concerning us, and they watch over us and have us in their keeping." (*Gospel Truth,* comp. Jerreld L. Newquist [Salt Lake City: Deseret Book Co., 1974], pp. 3–4.)

Elder Marvin J. Ashton helped us understand what is necessary to develop friendships: "For a few moments enjoy with me some very simple yet powerful recent conversations I've had in seeking the true significance of friendship. I asked an eight-year-old girl, 'Who is your best friend?' 'My mommie,' she replied. 'Why?' 'Because she is nice to me.'

"A priest-age young man was asked the same question. 'My bishop.' 'Why?' 'Because he listens to us guys.'

" . . . A 13-year-old boy: 'My Scoutmaster.' 'Why?' 'He does everything with us.'

"A prisoner: 'The chaplain.' 'Why?' 'He believes me. He even believed me sometimes when he shouldn't have.'

"A husband: 'My wife.' 'Why?' 'Because she is the best part of me.'" ("What Is a Friend?" *Ensign*, January 1973, p. 43.)

From these comments, we can conclude that friendship is earned. Would you be willing to save a friend? Can you tell when a friend feels friendless, dejected, and hungry—like Wilbur, bad enough to fall down in a manure pile and sob? Some people do that, you know—probably not in a manure pile in the barnyard like Wilbur the pig, but in the waste and filth of the world because they feel worthless and good-for-nothing.

The following poem helps us understand our need to lift others out of the world and into the light of Christ:

My Friend

My friend, I stand in judgment now
And feel that you're to blame somehow.
On earth I walked with you each day,
But never did you point the way.

You knew the Lord in truth and glory,
But never did you tell His story.
My knowledge, then, was very dim.
You could have led me straight to Him!

Though we lived together on the earth,
You never mentioned the second birth;
And now I stand with joys deferred
Because you failed to share His word.

You taught me many things, it's true.
I called you friend and trusted you!
But I figure now how much I lost.
You could have saved me such a cost.

We walked by day and talked by night,
And yet you showed me not the light.
You let me live, and love, and die.
You knew how much I'd lose on high.

Yes—I did call you "friend" in life
And trusted you through joy and strife.
And yet on coming to the end,
I cannot call you now "my friend"!
(Authorship unknown)

When Robert Louis Stevenson was asked the secret of his radiant, useful life, he responded simply, "I had a friend." I pray that each of us will give of ourselves to others, for that is one of the best presents we can give: the gift of self. Charlotte was right when she said, "By helping you, perhaps I was trying to lift up my life a trifle. Heaven knows anyone's life can stand a little of that."

Randall C. Bird taught seminary for more than twenty years and is now manager of seminary curriculum in the Church Educational System. He is the stake president of the Layton Utah East Stake. Brother Bird and his wife, Carla, are the parents of six children.

6

BEING FRIENDS WITH YOUNG MEN

Lisa H. Olsen

The sun setting behind the mountains cast a golden glow on the outdoor arena. Spotlights highlighted the competition floor as the audience sat silently. Male competitors waited nervously backstage, sizing up the competition. It was the perfect night for the international contest! Weeks of eliminations had narrowed the field to three athletes. I waited quietly and whispered to my friends, trying to decide which routine Richard would use for freestyle competition.

The announcer broke the tension: "Welcome, ladies and gentlemen. Our first competitor is Richard Glazier, representing the United States."

Just then Richard appeared at the top of a beautifully groomed hill and waved to his cheering fans. With confidence he descended to the competition floor. His face was serious; he wanted this title. Saluting the judges to acknowledge the beginning of his routine, he placed his hands on the edge of the apparatus. All eyes followed closely as he pulled himself onto the trampoline and began to flop and turn like a suffocating fish.

With one last, great spasm, Richard landed perfectly upright and began to bounce, his arms held in perfectly choreographed unison. Richard then fell on his back, bounced back up, and attempted a toe-touch. After a few somersaults he jumped up, still swaying from the motion of the trampoline, and saluted the judges, who held up their score cards: perfect tens! The audience—all eight of us—broke out cheering, knowing that Richard had clearly done a jump so ugly that neither Trent nor John could possibly equal it. It was summer again, time for the ugly jump contests in Mark's backyard.

As I remember such experiences with my friends, I am convinced that I had a highly unique (albeit a little strange) group of outstanding friends. I was especially lucky to count among them many young men who were "just friends." I am now thirty, and I work with teenagers daily. I watch many young women struggle with identity and work to figure out how to fit in.

As a teenager I felt I had a lot going for me: I had a wonderful family, I maintained good grades, I had good friends, and I was very involved in school extracurricular activities. But I still felt like a social misfit. I had plenty of girlfriends, and, just like many of them, my thoughts frequently turned to boys. Also, I worried too much about appearance because I didn't look like all the popular girls. I had naturally curly hair that was impossible to control, I wore braces from seventh grade until I was a junior in high school, I wore glasses (I should say I was *supposed* to wear glasses, because I never put them on at school), I didn't have much fashion sense (but neither did anyone else in the early eighties), and I didn't live in the chic part of town. Because of my exploding curly hair, boys would joke and call me "peach fuzz." When I cut my hair very short, it made me look about forty, so the boys started to call me "Miss Mature" and thought they were pretty funny.

When I turned sixteen, I thought boys would be able to see beyond my appearance and ask me out, but this was not the case. Instead, I was a very disappointed girl on my seventeenth birthday when I was still waiting for my first date. I had spent far too much desire and worry on wanting to date, and I knew that something had to change: me. I had to adjust my attitude and outlook. If boys weren't going to ask me out, then I was going to make them my friends. This proved to be one of the best resolves I ever made.

I also learned that Church leaders and General Authorities wanted me to make friends with young men and relax on the romance. For example, President Spencer W. Kimball specifically advised: "Dating and especially steady dating in the early teens is most hazardous. It distorts the whole picture of life. It deprives the youth of worthwhile and rich experiences; it limits friendships; it reduces the acquaintance which can be so valuable in selecting a partner for time and eternity." (*The Teachings of Spencer W. Kimball,* ed. Edward L. Kimball [Salt Lake City: Bookcraft, 1982], p. 289.) Steady dating limits friendships! Had I been a frequent dater in high school, I would have missed out on wonderful *friendships* with Steve, McKay, Jon, Scott, Dave, Paul, and of course the ugly jumpers.

Steve was the junior class president. He worked to make me an honorary member of student government; I had run for office every year but was never elected, so it was a thrill to still be involved somehow. Because I was an artist, he put me on every dance committee to work on decorations. During planning stages and the late decorating nights, I formed great friendships with many people. Steve was constantly inviting me and my friends Sara and Joanne to all his parties. McKay and Jon were friends I made through A Cappella who became like big brothers to me. Dave and Paul were best buddies I met while on the seminary council. And then there was Scott. I don't even remember the classes we had together or the things we talked about; I just remember that he was my knight in shining armor on the day of the junior prom. As with other dances, I had worked for hours on the decorations for this prom but was dateless. Scott had not planned on going to the prom because he was a senior, but, knowing how hard I had worked and how much I wanted to go to the prom, he came to my door one hour after the prom had started and whisked me to the dance. We had a great time—as friends.

I was also lucky to have three wonderful girlfriends: Ruth, Joanne, and Sara, who were all from my ward. Somehow we later merged with the ugly jumpers, John, Rich, and Mark. Sara described our friendships this way: "I looked at my guys as my friends, not as potential romances. They were like brothers but closer to our own age. They were the good boys next door. It was more fun to go with them as friends than to have a tantalizing romance, even if such a thing were possible."

Besides, romances make you worried, and you try to impress. We didn't entertain physical attractions, so we didn't feel inhibited. This attitude was more conducive to friendship.

One evening, while I was serving at a girlfriend's wedding reception, Mark, Rich, and John came into the kitchen to keep me company. As I wrote in my journal: "They came and sat in the kitchen with us for over an hour. Rich and John had a cream puff stuffing contest: Rich ate a whole cream puff in one bite, then John put two in his mouth, and then Rich stuffed in three in one bite. It was disgusting! After the reception we went up to Haley's house to order pizza and watch *North Avenue Irregulars*. As we were leaving, our attention turned to a sheet cake. Rich grabbed a piece with his bare hands and put the whole thing in his mouth. John, not wanting to be outdone, shoved in two whole pieces. Then Rich stuffed in three and kissed Haley, smearing frosting all over her face. As if things couldn't get worse, John actually put four pieces in his mouth. Typical." Obviously, these boys weren't out to impress us.

Our group spent endless hours together. As we all look back, we remember that most of our time was spent talking. It was fun to listen to the guys open up and actually share their thoughts and feelings (I never experienced that on a first, or second, or third date). These talks were especially memorable when we would go up on Mark's roof for what we called a "roof sit," a long night of only talking, or when we would ride the mopeds to the temple grounds to talk. Other great memories include: making movies and editing them at Mark's father's studio; the girls kidnapping John, tying him up, blindfolding him, putting him on the doorstep of a girl he liked, ringing the bell, and leaving John behind (it later went down in history as our group's best practical joke); passing out copies of the Book of Mormon in Las Vegas; enjoying formal Christmas dinners at Ruth Ann's house; and trying to take over the world in a game of Risk (our group's official game). These young men were the best friends I could have ever asked for. I treasure their friendships—they even helped me form an idea about the kind of man I would eventually like to marry.

Our modern-day prophet and the General Authorities have given other specific advice on friendships: "In cultures where dating is appropriate, do not date until you are sixteen years old. Not all teenagers need to date or even want to. Many young people do not date during their teen years, because they are not interested, do not have opportunities, or simply want to delay forming serious relationships. Good friendships can be developed at every age." (*For the Strength of Youth* [pamphlet, 1990], p. 7.) I don't know if you fit into one of the mentioned categories; when I was a teenager, I fit into the "do not have opportunities" category. Modern prophets have reminded us that "good friendships can be developed at every age." There is a time and a season for everything (see Ecclesiastes 3:1): now is the time for you to concentrate on *friendships* with young men.

A Telling Survey

My friend Scott Simmons and I teach at the same high school and decided to conduct a small survey to see if our students believed that friendships can be formed with someone of the opposite sex. We found that young men value friendships with young women and feel that they have a lot to gain from these friendships. Here are several examples of what they said:

"Same-sex friendships, at least with guys, are usually limited to fun, and rarely do they communicate real feelings as do relationships with girls."

"I tend to be better friends with girls because I can hang around them and not get into trouble. They keep me from doing the wrong thing. They keep me in line."

"I have a lot of female friends. They're fun to be around. You can talk to them, and yet if you wanted to get closer you could, but you don't have to because there's no pressure."

"Same-sex friendships: you share more of the same interests. Opposite-sex (girl) friendships: you can talk to them about things that you can't tell other people."

"I find it's more enjoyable to be in the presence of people of the opposite sex. You try to please them more."

"One of my best friends in the world is a girl. She lives in Tennessee. We were good friends and did a lot of things together. People at school always thought we were going out. We had an understanding of each other. We got along very well, but we weren't attracted to each other. When I moved to Utah, my bishop said it was sad I was leaving her."

The young women in our survey also felt that they had a lot to gain from friendships with young men:

"You could be friends with a brother or father and also just a friend. You don't have to date to have guy friends."

"With the opposite sex, I don't feel obligated to call or do something with them because they aren't mad if you don't."

"A friendship of the opposite sex can improve your communication skills."

"Sometimes they make the best kind of friendships. Guys know more about other guys than you do, and sometimes they can tell you which ones to watch out for and stay away from. They always are more fun to talk to than most girls. Guys don't whine as much either."

"You can always trust guys. Girls tell all, but guys will respect you and what you say. Friendships with guys are better."

"It bugs me when people think a relationship *always* has to be romantic. I have had friends of the opposite sex for years, and we have had so much fun together mainly because we weren't involved romantically."

"My best friend is a guy. We can totally talk about everything and anything, and we have the best time together. I wouldn't want to be more than friends with him because it would ruin the awesome friendship we have."

Two other questions on our survey were also very revealing. Girls, what follows are the frank, unaltered perspectives of the sixty-three young men ages 14 to 18 who we surveyed. We asked: "What are the three most important qualities of a friend?" and "What are the three most important qualities of someone you want to date?" The top ten qualities in each category were:

Friendship	*Someone you want to date*
1. Trustworthy	1. Looks
2. Honest	2. Good Personality
3. Humor	3. Humor
4. Nice	4. Fun to be with
5. Loyal/devoted	5. High standards
6. Good listener	6. Nice
7. Fun to be with	7. Compatible
8. Good personality	8. Honest
9. Helpful	9. Good attitude
10. Friendly	10. Intelligent

As I looked at the two lists, the number-one qualities struck me as demonstrating the greatest contrast between the two types of relationships. In friendship, *trust* is first, and in dating, *looks* received the top response. However, *looks* is not listed on the friendship top-ten list and in fact was mentioned on only two of the surveys. Young women know all too well that the girls we think are popular or asked out a lot are often the girls perceived to be beautiful. It is unfair that we make such comparisons and base how we feel about ourselves on something over which we have little control.

We cannot change our physical characteristics given at birth, so let's relax and concentrate on developing an attractive personality. President Gordon B. Hinckley said to the young women of the Church: "Some of you may feel that you are not as attractive and beautiful and glamorous as you would like to be. Rise above any such feelings, cultivate the light you have within you, and it will shine through as a radiant expression that will be seen by others." ("The Light Within You," *Ensign*, May 1995, p. 99.) Young women possess the power to cultivate the qualities and characteristics of a good friend, and those qualities will help bring about the radiant expression President Hinckley is talking about.

Choose Young Male Friends Wisely

"Iron sharpeneth iron; so a man sharpeneth the countenance of his friend" (Proverbs 27:17).

I often hear about the influence young women have on young men, such as the young man in the survey who said, "They keep me in line." In my life, I have been profoundly affected by my friendships with men. They have opened my eyes to a new world I might have never discovered before marriage. Men have a different perspective on life and can add dimension to our perspectives. So, how do you decide which boys should be your friends? My first instinct and advice is to tell you to *relax* and let friendship take its course. Don't force friendship; it will develop naturally.

President David O. McKay once asked his friend George Q. Morris (who later served on the Council of the Twelve) how one could know if he or she was in love. Although he was speaking of marriage, as a teenager I changed Elder Morris's words a little to apply to choosing friends. "'My mother once said that if you meet a [person] in whose presence you feel a desire to achieve, who inspires you to do your best, and to make the most of yourself, such a young [person] is worthy of your love and is awakening love in your heart" (*Man May Know For Himself*, comp. Clare Middlemiss [Salt Lake City: Deseret Book Co., 1969], p. 217). When I was developing friendships with guys, I would ask myself, "How do I feel in his presence?" and "What do I want to do with my life when I am with him?"

Here's a goofy example. John was one of my best friends. When we met, I was a "chain chewer" who went through at least two packages of gum a day. My friends would always comment on my chewing habits. One evening, John called to see if I could go with him to a friend's wedding reception. As we walked through the line, I was shocked to see that everyone in the line was chewing gum. As the bride talked to us, we could see a big wad of gum going from cheek to cheek.

We sat down at a table, and John tried discreetly to talk about this gum-chewing phenomenon in the line. I was so disgusted with how it looked that I told John, "I'm never chewing gum again!" John just laughed and said, "I triple-dog dare you to never chew gum again your entire life!" I pulled all the packages of gum out of my purse and handed them over with a determined "You're on!" That was ten years ago, and in those ten years gum has never touched my lips. It was probably the triple-dog dare that made me want to do it. John still remembers his challenge and asks each time we talk if I'm still gumless.

General Authorities are very mindful to teach youth to choose their friends carefully. This would be especially wise as you select male friends. Elder Hugh W. Pinnock said, "Associate with young men and young women who are straight and who will assist you to be responsible. Help your friends decide to go on missions, to attend Church meetings, and to enjoy righteous activities." ("Your Personal Checklist for a Successful Eternal Flight," *Ensign*, November 1993, p. 41.) Elder Richard G. Scott echoed his thoughts: "One of the hardest things for you to recognize is how truly strong you already are and how others silently respect you. We have great confidence in you. You don't need to compromise your standards to be accepted by good friends." ("Making the Right Choices," *Ensign*, November 1994, p. 37.)

An experience with my friend Mark illustrates this. In January 1985 I was feeling sad because Sara, Ruth, and Joanne had all left for Washington, D.C., for four months. I wrote in my journal:

> It's weird not having girlfriends to talk to. Now my closest friends left are all boys. It seems like everyone in the world has a boy/girlfriend, but not Lisa. What is wrong with me? Why me? Anyway, today I was feeling sorry for myself, having a pity party. John called me and cheered me up. Just as I hung up Mark called. We talked for a long time about how I felt. He wasn't feeling so hot either, so he told me his concerns. We worry about the same things. Anyway, at the end of the conversation he was telling me what he does when he gets upset, and he challenged me to do it for a week and to read the book *As a Man Thinketh*. Included in his challenge was journal writing every night. I took on the challenge. It goes like this:
>
> Mornings: 10 minutes of prayer, read 2 chapters from the standard works and 10–20 pages from a book about a prophet's life.
>
> Afternoons: 5 minutes of prayer.
>
> Evenings: 10 minutes of prayer, read patriarchal blessing, write in journal.
>
> He also talked a lot about service. He challenged me to a week, so I'm doing it! Mark made my day. He's seriously the best friend I have right now.

Choose carefully young male friends who will challenge you constantly (in a fun and nonthreatening way) to improve the quality of your life.

Develop Trust by Respecting Differences

"A friend . . . sticketh closer than a brother" (Proverbs 18:24).

There are differences in ideas on friendship between the sexes. It is important for us as women to recognize that men act differently. In order to be a friend who sticks "closer than a brother," it is important to respect these differences. It is interesting to me to compare the insight of my teenage friends with what professional researchers have learned. There are differences in the development of adolescent friendships:

Three phases of friendship have been described for adolescent girls (Douvan & Adelson, 1966). In the early phase, age 11 to 13, friendship is based on activity. Friends are people who do things together. In the middle phase, age 14 to 16, friendship is based on loyalty and trust. Friends are people you can confide in, people who will not betray you to others. During this period, anxiety about friendship and fears of rejection are especially strong. These fears are observed in both boys and girls, but girls express feelings of jealousy and rejection more openly (Coleman, 1980). In the third phase, age 17 and beyond, personality and shared interests figure more prominently in friendships. Anxiety about rejection is reduced, and older adolescents place greater value on the individual qualities of a friend. Friendships among older adolescents are characterized by greater openness and mutual understanding (Bell, 1981; Berndt, 1982). For boys, the pattern appears to be somewhat different. First, the movement away from activity-based friendships is less marked. Second, anxiety about rejection is not as intense nor as prolonged. Third, the level of intimacy and mutual understanding among same-sex male friendships is not as great as for same-sex female friendships (Bell, 1981; Coleman, 1980). (Barbara M. Newman and Philip R. Newman, *Adolescent Development*, pp. 231–32.)

I love what my student Kim said about friendships with boys: "I have more boyfriends than girlfriends. I have always had more boyfriends than girlfriends. It is very possible that the majority of the responsibility lies on the girl's shoulders. She has to be outgoing and willing to do things that might scare her or may not seem fun to her." Our idea of a fun time (for example, let's do lunch!) may not exactly be a guy's idea of a fun time. Young men are naturally activity oriented. I would recommend that you use good judgment and caution if you seem worried about an idea. Sometimes they have been doing an activity a lot longer than you have and have a lot of experience behind them.

Doing something that you don't normally do can create great memories. I remember well one afternoon when my friends Mark and Rich were in another one of what they called their "Huck Finn" moods. They came over to my house without any warning and told me to go get on a swimsuit because we were going to a "swimming hole." We drove up the canyon, stopped at a popular campground, and walked to some train tracks above the river. I laughed at their swimming trunks because they had tied ropes around their waists (a nice touch). Rich and Mark climbed up to the train tracks, took a big jump, screamed all the way down, and landed in the river. They sparked in me a sense of adventure, so when they said it was my turn, I climbed up, looked quickly down, and took a flying jump. Rich and Mark took my picture to prove that I actually did it. Now, that's something I would have never thought of doing with my girlfriends.

Through activities and shared experiences, young men develop a trust in you, and they will eventually begin to open up and share their feelings. Don't pry or expect them to share personal things early in the friendship (like girls who quickly reveal their whole life story). You must be careful not to do anything to break that trust and not to share the personal conversations with anyone. One young man commented to me that "you can tell boys anything, and they won't tell anyone. But if you tell a girl something, it will be around the school in seconds." One of my girl students feels the same: "You can always trust guys. Girls tell all, but guys will respect you and what you say. Friendships with guys can be better."

My guy friends always valued my opinion because I could help them see the feminine perspective. One evening I realized that I had "arrived" with a great friendship. I was out with two of my friends, both boys, and it was time to go home. We were parked in my driveway talking about our favorite topics of conversation: the differences between boys and girls, and boys or girls who we were interested in dating. One boy was particularly confused about the signals a girl was sending him. He turned to me and, without thinking carefully, said, "Lisa, if you were a girl, what would you do?" My first reaction was to slug him; he retaliated and punched back, asking what was wrong with me. The other guy was really laughing hard. We all started laughing when it dawned on him that he actually said to me "if you were a girl." We had all come to a point in our friendship that, regardless of being boys or girls, we were *friends* first, friends who would help each other out no matter what.

Our boy friends often rescued us emotionally. These same two young men were knights in shining armor to us. Sara remembers a date that was planned with a boy she liked. She had dressed up and was very excited for the date. She waited and waited for him to come. After two hours, she realized that she had actually been stood up. Very disappointed, she went into her bedroom to change into something casual. When she went back into the living room, the doorbell rang. It was Mark and Rich. They said, "We're here to take you out on a date!" She had absolutely no idea how they found out what had happened. They piled into Mark's father's fancy car and had an even better evening than she would have had with her date. Only a friend you love and trust can pick up your spirits so well.

Express Love and Concern
"A friend loveth at all times" (Proverbs 17:17).

My favorite example of a friend loving at all times is a story of two sisters, their brother, and a special friend. The sisters were Mary and Martha, their brother was Lazarus, and the friend was Christ. The first time the sisters met Christ was when he visited their village. Martha invited him to her house. Her sister Mary was waiting at home.

"Now it came to pass, as they went, that he entered into a certain village: and a certain woman named Martha received him into her house. And she had a sister called Mary, which also sat at Jesus' feet, and heard his word. But Martha was cumbered about much serving, and came to him, and said, Lord, dost thou not care that my sister hath left me to serve alone? bid her therefore that she help me. And Jesus answered and said unto her, Martha, Martha, thou art careful and troubled about many things: But one thing is needful: and Mary hath chosen that good part, which shall not be taken away from her." (Luke 10:38–42.)

It's interesting to me that when Christ is received into the home, Martha is more worried about the condition of the home and about preparing the meal than Mary is. Mary is involved in getting to know her company. Christ taught Mary.

Christ was an important friend to this family. When their brother Lazarus died, they immediately called for Christ, their Savior and their friend. They knew that he possessed the power to heal but also that he had the power to comfort.

"Then when Mary was come where Jesus was, and saw him, she fell down at his feet, saying unto him, Lord, if thou hadst been here, my brother had not died. When Jesus therefore saw her weeping, and the Jews also weeping which came with her, he groaned in the spirit, and was troubled. And said, Where have ye laid him? They said unto him, Lord, come and see. Jesus wept. Then said the Jews, Behold how he loved him!" (John 11:32–36.)

Christ then went to the grave of Lazarus and commanded him to live. He loved Mary and Martha and was a perfect friend to them.

From ugly jump contests to the last-minute junior prom, I have fond memories of my male *friends* and will be forever grateful for their friendships and love. They helped me to balance my life with interesting and worthwhile activities and ideas. I wish you newfound happiness as you develop friendships with young men. The time will eventually come for choosing just one, so work hard to create a million happy teenage memories with no regrets!

Lisa H. Olsen *served a mission in Geneva, Switzerland, has worked for several years with the Especially for Youth program, and currently teaches art at Timpview High School in Provo, Utah. She is married to Brent Olsen, and they are the parents of a son, Cole.*

7

BEING FRIENDS WITH YOUNG WOMEN

R. Scott Simmons

I don't know about you, but when I was younger I loved to build forts and huts. We had tree huts, hay huts, dugouts, and so on. Everything from cardboard to an abandoned Chevy was employed in making these modern miracles of construction. Our tools usually came from Dad's garage. Our dads were very generous, especially when they were not around. We would move in after we were sure that our fort would not collapse.

This assumption of safety came through a series of highly scientific tests, such as the hammer throw. I would look at my friend and say, "Make sure you duck. You know what happened last time." To which he would reply, "Why do I always have to stand in front?" Then the count down would begin: 5, 4, 3—hey, wait a minute, the wind blew it down again." At this point we aborted the hammer throw, and reconstruction began with a comment such as, "Maybe this time we should use nails."

We decorated our forts with items gathered from around the

home. We usually took things that Mom would not miss. The following items were usually standard in any hut: A candle, used for light, cooking, and just to satisfy a general fascination with fire. Blankets and pillows for sleeping out, although this never happened because of a common childhood phobia called "fear of sleeping out in a fort when it's dark and you're not sure if the locks you installed will keep monsters out." A two-year supply of cookies, pork and beans, pickles, honey, chili, candy, bandages, and other necessities gathered from our parents' food storages. A knife, for throwing. The traditional Scout mess kit, for eating (if this was unavailable, several of Mom's china dishes and good silverware would do; after all, she did not use them anyway). Comic books and a newspaper; the comic books for intellectual stimulation, the newspaper for patching holes in the walls and starting fires that we usually put out in time, without the help of the fire department. A pair of scissors, for cutting off each others' singed hair after fires. Finally, the crowning decoration, which no fort or hut could be without: a big sign that proclaimed in bold letters, "NO GIRLS ALLOWED."

I have a sister who is a year younger than I am. Through much of my adolescent life, it seemed like she had to go wherever and do whatever I did. Now, this might not seem so bad; after all, how much harm could one little girl do? The problem was that my sister suffered from a childhood disease common to girls which was known to boys as "girlfriends." Mere mention of the word would send any young boy looking for a better place to hide.

What is so bad about "girlfriends"? Don't boys have friends? The answer is yes, boys have friends, usually a best friend and occasionally two. The problem with girls was that they always traveled in packs. No boy likes to be outnumbered. So, to eliminate the problem, we simply avoided them at all costs. Girls or anything to do with girls—especially "girlfriends"—was strictly taboo.

However, this was easier said than done. The girls were persistent. No matter what we did to drive them away, they always came back. They would usually return with their secret weapon: cookies. They always seemed to know just when our two-year supply ran out. With cookies in hand, they would begin to inflict upon us cruel and unusual punishment, which I know the Geneva Convention would have outlawed.

The torture went like this: one girl would take a big bite of a cookie and say, "Mm-m-m, these must be the best cookies Mom has ever made." Another girl, also taking a bite, would add, "You're right, and look how many there are. Too bad we don't have anyone to share them with." At this point we would break under the extreme pressure, and negotiations would begin.

Negotiations were simple. We would yell, "Give us some cookies." They would yell back, "Let us in." At which point we would yell, "Okay." With negotiations concluded, they took us prisoner and commandeered our fort.

Before we knew it, there were curtains, giggling, dolls, giggling, a table cloth, giggling, cleaning, giggling, and no more cookies. When the cookies ran out, we quickly made our escape with our "NO GIRLS ALLOWED" sign in hand and plans for a new girl-proof fortress.

It seems like we learned growing up that girls were nothing but a big pain and something we avoided unless they had something of value that we wanted. As we grew older, cookies became kisses, and negotiations continued. As usual, when the kisses ran out we made our escape with sign in hand.

I may not have all the answers, but I would like to suggest some things that may help as you try to bridge the gap from "NO GIRLS ALLOWED" to "girlfriends." For these suggestions I have drawn on my own experiences and those of my students.

First, you need to understand that young ladies are different. Right now you're probably thinking, "They surely are. They are about as weird as you can get, and what's up with all that giggling."

Hold it! I do not mean different as in weird. I mean different as in not like boys. Let me explain.

Generally young ladies are more gentle, kind, loving, and compassionate. Young men are a little rougher around the edges. This is just an example. It would take a separate chapter just to explore these differences. Besides, the important thing is not to know all the differences. The important thing is to understand that there *are* differences.

As one of my students said, "Young men just need to understand that they don't understand." If you can do that, you are halfway there. As the writer of Proverbs counseled, "With all thy getting get understanding" (Proverbs 4:7). When asked what blessing he would have from the Lord, Solomon asked for "an understanding heart" (1 Kings 3:9). "And God gave Solomon wisdom and understanding exceeding much, and largeness of heart, even as the sand that is on the sea shore" (1 Kings 4:29). Seek to understand.

Second, learn to listen. Almost every young lady I talked to said, "I wish guys would just listen." I discovered that there are three ways you can listen.

The first and most obvious way is with your ears. To do this you simply have to be within hearing range.

The second way to listen is with your eyes. Have you ever tried to talk to someone who is not looking at you?

The third and probably most difficult way to listen is with your heart. This happens when you not only hear what the person is saying but you feel it too. To do this you really need the help of the Spirit.

In my office I have a Dennis the Menace cartoon that shows Dennis's mom wiping some tears from his eyes. The caption reads, "I'm OK. I just felt so bad for Joey that I helped him cry." That is listening with your heart. The Savior did the same thing in John 11:32–36. Learn to listen.

Next, be willing to talk about how you feel. Typically young ladies share their feelings freely. This is their way of working through things. Young men, on the other hand, keep more to themselves. Can you imagine this conversation in a locker room after a football game?

Phil: "Great game, John."

John: "You really think so?"

Phil: "I really do. I just love the way you throw the ball. In fact, John, you're just about the best football player I know."

John: "Thanks, Phil. That means a lot to hear you say that. I think you're awesome too."

Sound kind of ridiculous? That's because it does not happen. Yet, if you are going to be friends with young ladies, you need to be willing to share. Young ladies want to know how you feel, especially about spiritual things. You do not have to be sappy, just say how you feel. Some of the best conversations I have had with young ladies are about the gospel. Share your feelings.

Fourth, be honest. Without reservation, every young lady I talked to mentioned honesty. This is also important to the Lord. Listen to your *For the Strength of Youth* pamphlet: "Be honest with yourself and others, including the Lord. Honesty with yourself brings peace and self-respect. When you are honest with others, you build a foundation for friendship and trust." (P. 9.) Did you catch that honesty is the foundation of friendship? The Book of Mormon describes the people of Ammon as "perfectly honest and upright in all things" (Alma 27:27). Be honest.

Fifth, be a builder. One thing that many young ladies mentioned as an important quality was humor. They like young men who are fun to be with. However, they would always add that it is never funny to cut someone down. So much of the humor we see in the world today tears others down. This is one characteristic of the people in the great and spacious building Lehi saw in his dream: "They were in the attitude of mocking and pointing their fingers towards those who had come at and were partaking of the fruit" (1 Nephi 8:27). The prophet Alma counseled us: "And again I say unto you, is there one among you that doth make a mock of his brother, or that heapeth upon him persecutions? Wo unto such an one, for he is not prepared, and the time is at hand that he must repent or he cannot be saved!" (Alma 5:30–31.)

Do not make fun of people; in doing so, you make fun of the one in whose image they were created. Instead, look for ways to build people up. Have you ever noticed what young ladies typically do when they greet each other? Well, after they hug they compliment each other. One will say, "I love your hair," and the other will respond, "I love your outfit." They are building. If you want to make friends fast, learn to give genuine compliments. In a world where people are constantly being torn down, we need builders. Be a builder.

Sixth, control your passions. As you become friends with young ladies, there will be a temptation to become intimate. One of the fastest ways to ruin a friendship is to become physical. Listen to Alma's counsel to his son Shiblon: "See that ye bridle all your passions, that ye may be filled with love" (Alma 38:12). Notice it does not say to kill your passions but only to control them. If you look at the resulting blessing, you see that you will be filled with love. If you want to really be able to love, do not get physical and do control your passions.

Okay, let's review:

1. Understand that young ladies are different.
2. Learn to listen.
3. Be willing to talk about your feelings.
4. Be honest.
5. Be a builder.
6. Bridle your passions.

Wow, that is quite a list. Does it seem a bit overwhelming? Well, it can be easier than you think. Let me now suggest some ways you can acquire these values.

First, learn from your mom. You have a great source of information right in your own home. Now, if the thought of talking to your mom makes you cringe, look at Alma 53:20–21: "And they were all young men, and they were exceedingly valiant for courage, and also for strength and activity; but behold, this was not all—they were men who were true at all times in whatsoever thing they were entrusted. Yea, they were men of truth and soberness, for they had been taught to keep the commandments of God and to walk uprightly before him."

What do you think of these guys? How would you like that to be a description of you? "Exceedingly valiant for courage" kind of has a ring to it, don't you think? Where do you suppose these young men learned to be like that: summer sports camp? Guess again—look at Alma 56:47. "Now they never had fought, yet they did not fear death; and they did think more upon the liberty of their fathers than they did upon their lives; yea, they had been taught by their mothers, that if they did not doubt, God would deliver them." Who taught them? That's right, their moms! If you want to be like the stripling warriors, learn from your mom.

One day while I was washing the car, my mom came out to ask me a question. I'm not sure why, but I asked her if she had time to talk. She said she did and asked what I wanted to talk about. I was not sure, so I asked her to tell me about her courtship with my dad. For two hours I washed the car while my mom told me the story. It was wonderful. I learned many things that day that helped me in my own courtship. It also brought me much closer to my mom.

Next, watch your dad. Talk to your mom, but watch your dad. Your mom has been training him for many years now, and chances are he's learned a thing or two about girlfriends. Your mom is his best friend. Is that a weird thought, that your mom and dad are friends? Not only friends, but best friends. Have you ever seen your mom and dad just goof around together? I love to watch my mom and dad.

One day my mom cut a picture of a shiny red Firebird out of a magazine and put it on the bulletin board. When I asked her about it, she commented that one day she was going to have one just like it. At the time she was driving "Old Blue," an old beat-up Chevy that we had put back together several times with baling wire and duct tape.

It was not long until we had saved enough money to replace Old Blue. It did not take Mom long to find a car like the one in her picture. The only problem was that it was out of our price range. After a week of trying to figure out how to pay for it, Mom finally decided her dream car would have to wait.

However, the next day Dad came home driving the new Firebird. You can imagine how thrilled and surprised my mom was to see her dream car. I'll never forget my dad's response when I questioned him about being able to afford the car. He said, "Son, look how it makes your mom feel to have a new car. I would have paid twice that much for her to feel that way." My dad is a builder.

If you do not have a father or if your father is struggling to live the gospel, look to a brother, uncle, grandfather, or any righteous priesthood holder.

Practice on your sister. I know what you're thinking: "That's it, you've finally crossed the line. There is no way I could ever be friends with my own sister." That is what I used to think. My sister used to drive me nuts, but then something occurred to change all that: We were sealed as a family in the temple. Although I was eleven, I remember the event as though it were yesterday.

My sister and I were led up to a sealing room in the Salt Lake Temple, where our parents and relatives were waiting for us. I still remember how I felt as I entered that sacred room and saw everyone I loved dressed in white. My sister and I were holding hands. It all felt so right, so good. We were then invited to join my mom and dad kneeling around a sacred altar, where we joined hands. Joining hands intensified the feeling of love. I felt as if I was getting a small taste of what it would be like in the celestial kingdom.

The sealer then pronounced those sacred words that bound my family together for eternity. As we left the room, I kept looking at my sister. Somehow she was different; for the first time, she was truly my sister. I remember putting my arm around her and saying, "This means we're forever." From then on our relationship was different. Oh, we still had our struggles, but knowing that we would be together forever gave me a greater desire to work through them.

Remember that we are all brothers and sisters, a forever family of our heavenly parents. If you learn to be friends with your immediate sister, you will find it easier to be friends with your gospel sisters. If you do not have a sister, practice on someone who is as close, like a cousin or neighbor. My sister is one of my best friends, and in many ways she is my hero. I am constantly trying to keep up with her Christlike example.

When I was at college, I found I had even more sisters. At Brigham Young University they broke us up into family home evening groups consisting of several apartments of guys and several apartments of girls. We referred to the girls as our family home evening sisters. I had some wonderful relationships with them, and some of my best practice learning how to be friends with young ladies came through experiences with these sisters. From them I learned many qualities of real friendship.

All right, it's time to get rid of your sign or paint a new one that says "Girls Allowed." Begin to acquire the attributes of friendship now, and one day it will happen: You will fall in love and marry. If you do it right, you will marry your best friend.

R. Scott Simmons teaches seminary at Timpview High School in Provo, Utah, and has recorded several talk tapes. In the fall of 1996 he will be teaching religion at Brigham Young University and working on an advanced degree. He and his wife, Nancy, live in Highland, Utah.

8

BEING FRIENDS IN TIMES OF TROUBLE

Stephen Jason Hall

The mighty whirl of the helicopter began to die down, and the doors flew open. The paramedics from Life Flight handed me off to the nurses and doctors of the ER at St. Mary's Hospital in Grand Junction, Colorado. With my dad at my side, I was taken into the trauma unit, where I was most certainly the center of attention. The team was doing a barrage of tests, checking my heart, my lungs, my eyes, ears, and nose. X-rays were done as well as a blood analysis. As time wore on and the doctors confirmed that my physical condition was stable, the atmosphere lightened a bit and I became the subject of a new set of tests designed to discern how much sensitivity and movement I had lost as a result of a diving accident a few short hours before at Lake Powell, Utah.

The doctor approached me with a small metal instrument that was sharp on one end and dull on the other. He explained to me that he was going to poke me with different sides of this instrument and I was to indicate if I felt the sharp or dull end or anything at all.

I watched the doctor proceed up my foot to my ankle—nothing. I saw him slowly move from my ankle to my knee—still nothing. I wanted to feel something so badly it hurt. I was concentrating with all my might, hoping to feel the prick of his instrument. He continued from my knee to my hip and then from my hip through my midsection to my chest—nothing. It wasn't until he reached under my arm that I felt something. "I felt that! I felt that!" I yelled, so pleased that I had finally felt something. He completed the same test on the other side of my body with the same result, compiled his information, and then left.

A short time later, the doctor returned. With a somberness in his voice that I shall never forget, he explained that his diagnosis was confirmed: I had broken my neck and would never walk again. Although he was 99 percent sure, he said that there was one test left to further support this diagnosis. Soon I was off for a CT scan.

The CT scanner looks like a large, white tube. They slide you into the middle of the tube and take in-depth pictures of your body. As I lay in the middle of the tube, the technician explained that he would be in an adjacent room administering the scan and that I must remain completely still.

As I was lying there as still as I possibly could, the room got very quiet and very lonely. In fact, I realized that since my accident earlier that day this was the first time I had been alone. And being alone caused my mind to wander.

I began to wonder what it would be like to live my life in a wheelchair and what changes that would bring—and then real concern set in. I wondered, *Who will want to go to the games with a guy in a wheelchair? Who will date or go to the prom with a guy in a wheelchair? Who will want to just hang out on a Saturday night with a guy in a wheelchair? Who will be my friend?* The answer I received to this last question during the year following my accident has taught me much about friendship and what it truly means to be a friend. I learned that everyone has acquaintances, but only the blessed have friends. I learned that acquaintances and colleagues are a dime a dozen, but true friends are golden. I also learned that these true friends almost always have the same characteristics. If we are willing to use these characteristics as a benchmark, we will more easily be able to discern who our true friends are.

Perspective

After three months of inpatient stay at the hospital, which were filled with braces, surgery, respirators, and therapy, I was finally released and allowed to go home. The ensuing months taught me a lot about the importance perspective has in friendship.

Before my accident, I was very involved both at school and in my ward—much like most fifteen-year-olds. Athletics was a big part of that involvement. Many of my friends were fellow teammates. We would spend hour upon hour in the weight room, on the practice field, and around the track. Our entire relationship was centered around the games we were preparing to play. When we were together we talked about sports and we watched professionals play the games we dreamed we would one day be a part of, and when our time together was finished we would talk of the games and races that would fill our tomorrows.

Suddenly, after my accident, I found that we no longer had much to talk about. I could no longer join them in practice or battle with them in the crosstown rivalries. And, on top of that, most of these friends were not Latter-day Saints. For most of them, life ended with this life. They had very little concept of a heaven, much less of a resurrection. Those who did have some concept of a God or heaven could not understand how he could allow this tragedy to happen. Our relationships, although strong and important to me, were built on one plane: our athletics. When that plane was gone, there was no perspective to lend any strength to our friendship.

At the same time, I had many Latter-day Saint friends. Although we did not have athletics in common, much of what we did was physical. Dances, ward activities, and all the other daily physical activities teenagers fill their time with were a big part of our friendship. However, when the physical aspects of our relationship were gone, there was something eternal to give our friendship meaning. The fact that we know that there is a God, that his purpose is always for the best, and that there is a resurrection and a place where all ailments will be healed gave our friendship a breadth and depth that could endure the loss of one aspect of our friendship. This eternal perspective was essential to the continuity of our care and concern for each other.

This is not to say that our only friends should be Latter-day Saints. But we must realize that only relationships with perspective and an understanding of what is truly important will last. We must seek after relationships that will foster this perspective, and we must strive to be the kind of friend that endures forever.

I first met Kolette in my junior year at Brigham Young University. We became fast friends. As we began to date, our relationship started to become more and more special to both of us. We began to spend all our free time together. Whenever either of us had a few extra minutes, we searched for ways to spend those minutes in the company of the other. As our relationship grew, it became evident that a decision of marriage was most definitely in the future. People who were very close to Kolette began to ask her if she could really handle being married to someone in a wheelchair. Out of concern for her, they filled her mind with questions she had not yet dealt with. Suddenly, every time we were together she began to wonder if she could live her life with a man in a wheelchair, if she could be happy in a relationship in which the responsibility for everything from mowing the lawn to teaching the kids to play football would fall on her shoulders.

All of this questioning caused Kolette a lot of concern. But, as she took some time for private contemplation and sincere prayer, she found her answer. She learned that she was asking the wrong kinds of questions. The question that really mattered was, "Do I love Jason?" If she could answer that question affirmatively, then the answers to the other questions would come easily. She had to decide if she cared about what was essential about me: my spirit and my heart. Everything physical was secondary. She could deal with the fact that I couldn't stand if she knew she loved me.

Six months later we were married. We are happier now than we can ever remember. How grateful I am for my sweetheart, who chose to have an eternal perspective.

Sometimes when we choose the people who will fill our lives as friends, we are tempted to first answer the questions that Kolette was confronted with—but all those things are physical. We worry about who is the most popular, who has the most money, or who is the most beautiful. Because the eternal does not come naturally, we often look first to the captain of the football team or the head cheerleader as we try to find friends. Although there are plenty of football stars and homecoming queens who are wonderful people, when we seek friends we must first look at the hearts and souls of those we choose to be a part of our inner circle.

If we find people who are striving to live a righteous life, show a genuine concern and love for others, and have an eternal perspective, whether they are at the top or bottom of the social ladder, they will be friends to last a lifetime, come what may.

Sacrifice

Sacrifice is a crucial part of the equation as we work to find friends who are real and lasting. Friends who are willing to sacrifice for each other show that their relationship has importance and that other things previously thought to have importance no

longer do. Yet, this sacrifice has parameters. People who are willing to sacrifice their integrity, faith, or righteous living are most
assuredly not friends.

When I first left the hospital, I badly wanted to reenter high
school. I knew that my weak body and decreased stamina would
not allow me to return full-time, so I would only be able to attend
a few classes. At the same time, I had physical therapy to attend
from morning until early afternoon. This meant that if I was to attend school I would have to go to early-morning classes, then go
to therapy, and then return to school for the final hour of the day.

When I started back to school, my mother did all the driving.
She was always glad to do it, and she worked hard to balance her
schedule at home to make it work. But it began to take its toll on
her and on my younger brothers and sister. After a few months,
two of my close friends, Scott and Susie, noticed the effort it took
on my mother's part and the difficulty it caused for my family, so
they offered to pick me up and drop me off at home each day.
This task was not as simple or easy as it sounds. They would have
to get up early (sometimes only to wait for me), lift me in and out
of the car, and make sure my clothes looked just right and my
school supplies were all situated correctly—only to repeat the
whole process at the end of the day.

This was not easy or convenient for them. They stood to gain
nothing from completing the task. Yet they did it, not only driving me to school, but to activities, study groups, church affairs,
and even once to toilet-paper our teacher's yard. They never
complained or made me feel as though I was a burden. They
were always cheerful and happy to do it. They made me feel that
I was just another member of a carpool. They were willing to
sacrifice for me daily because they were truly my friends. Often
we think we know who our friends are, but when sacrifice is
necessary, we truly know.

I will not soon forget my first real backpacking adventure as
a young Boy Scout, before my accident. I had procrastinated
preparing for the event until just an hour before we were to

leave, so I didn't worry about what would be lightest or most simple to pack—I just packed. First I grabbed the tightly rolled sleeping bag and foam pad from the storage closet. Although I had never practiced rolling them myself, I figured it couldn't be too hard and that I could learn after we reached the campsite. After throwing some clothes in, I had to worry about food. Since I had no desire to eat anything dehydrated, I quickly ran to the pantry and grabbed four cans of Spaghettios and a six-pack of Sprite. I knew these items would be heavy, but I had to pack them only one way, and I was sure we'd have a garbage can nearby where I could throw away the empty cans. Finally, all packed and ready to go, I grabbed my brand-new hiking boots out of their box and ran out the door.

The five miles into camp weren't too bad. My backpack weighed a lot, but I was rested and made the trip without incident. Although my new boots made my feet tender in a few places, we had a wonderful time on the camp-out—but by the end of the weekend, those tender areas were blisters. And although the Spaghettios tasted good, there was no trash can to be found and I had to find a way to pack the empty cans out of the camp. Unfortunately, trash always seems to take up more room, so there was no longer any room on my backpack for the foam pad and it therefore ended up under my arm. The sleeping bag I packed out resembled the one I packed in only because they were the same color; it was so loosely rolled that it barely fit on top of my pack.

As we left that site, I was completely unprepared for the five miles that lay ahead. And it went from bad to worse. The blisters on my feet became so painful that I had to finish the trek with only one boot on. Not long after that, my loosely rolled sleeping bag unrolled so that one end was dragging through the mud; it looked more like a wedding veil than a sleeping bag. Needless to say, I was a sight—and I was beginning to lag way behind. It got bad enough that I was willing to endure any humiliation that asking for help might create. Each of the boys ahead, all of whom purported to be my friends, were too busy or preoccupied to help me—all except one.

Unlike me, Mark was prepared. His backpack looked great. Realizing that my packing job was probably unsalvageable at this stage of the game, he carried my foam pad and my garbage so that my sleeping bag would fit inside my backpack with my clothes. Mark's journey back to the vehicles was substantially more difficult than it needed to be. He was prepared, and I was not. But he was willing to endure a little pain to help me—because he was my friend.

It is easy to find friends who will be with us when the sun shines. What we must work diligently to do is find, and be, the kind of friends who are willing to make the sacrifices necessary to stick together when life gets stormy.

Encouragement

As we choose our friends, we also must work to find those who will give us the motivation and courage to do the difficult things we must do in order to progress. Often, we are more apt to act like water running down a hill: we take the path of least resistance. Although sometimes it is wrong, we want to take the easiest path simply because it is easiest. True friends help us avoid that syndrome and help us be trailblazers, people who are willing to do the hard things because it is the right thing to do.

When I came home from the hospital, I was scared to get back into my life at high school. I wanted to, but knowing I would have to do things differently from others and from how I had done them before scared me. Basketball games would come up and I was nervous to go, wondering where I would sit. Dances would come, and I wondered who I would interact with. Ward activities would come, and I was concerned how I could become a part of the group.

How grateful I am for friends like Topher and Dave. If any activity came up, they were at my door, ready to load me in their car. If we went to ball games, they would make sure I got lifted up to the upper decks so I could sit with the rest of the students and not with the parents below. All of this they did without ever being asked and without hesitation. In fact, sometimes it was done against my will. Sometimes I would get so concerned that I would not want to attend the activities at all, but this made no difference to Topher and Dave. They would show up at my door to take me whether I said I wanted to or not. They refused to let me miss any activity because of apprehension caused by my disability. And each time I would go against my will, the concern and nervousness would leave, and I would be grateful to have gone.

True friends are those like Dave and Topher who encourage us to do things, righteous things, that we may not otherwise do on our own. We must seek after those people who help us be righteous trailblazers and who help us to progress.

As we apply these criteria of perspective, sacrifice, and encouragement, we will find true friends we never knew or friends we forgot we knew. And in so doing, we probably will find that no one very often loves us more for who we are inside than our parents and our Savior. Although the Savior is perfect and our parents are not, both have the sincere love for us that helps them have an eternal perspective. Both have also made tremendous sacrifices for our well-being. Through sacrifice, our parents have clothed and fed us, taught and led us. And truly there is no greater sacrifice in recorded history than the one made in our behalf by our Savior, Jesus Christ. Finally, both our Savior and our parents encourage us to do righteous things we might not otherwise do. Sometimes against our will, they help us do things to make us better.

In essence, we must be choosy. We must avoid "here today, gone tomorrow" friends and make a conscious effort to find friends to last a lifetime and beyond. We will find a path that leads to joy and happiness as we consider eternal perspective, sacrifice, and encouragement when we ask ourselves, "Who will be my friend?"

Stephen Jason Hall *graduated from Brigham Young University, where he was president of BYUSA, the school's student service organization. He has had speaking engagements across the country and currently works as a financial planner in Salt Lake City. He is married to Kolette Coleman.*

9

BEING FRIENDS WITH THOSE
WHO ARE NOT
LATTER-DAY SAINTS

Ardeth Kapp

I t was in Seattle, at McDonald's, under the big arches, on a Saturday night around 9:30 P.M. Two young men and four young women were huddled over a table in the corner with a good supply of napkins covering a major portion of the entire table. What were they doing?

The following morning was fast and testimony meeting. Near the close of the meeting, a young man walked to the podium. I was a visitor in the ward and did not ask his name, but I shall never forget his message or the spirit in which he shared his feelings. He began with a broad grin and then glanced from the corner of his eye at his friend who had been sitting by him in the audience.

"Well," he said, leaning on one side of the pulpit and then the other, "my friend and I received a call last night around 9:15. It was one of the girls from school." He hesitated and then explained, "She said she and three of her girlfriends from school were at McDonald's and were talking about us and what we believed and how we are different. She said they wanted us to come to McDonald's and tell them how come we are different."

The young man's smile enlarged; he may have been thinking that the girls' request was a new approach to get a couple of young guys to meet them on a Saturday night. He continued, "We weren't doing anything anyway, so we thought, why not?" He paused a moment, and his countenance changed. "They were serious," he said. "They really did want to know what we believed and what makes us different."

He told how, in an effort to answer their many questions, he and his friend pulled a table to a corner of the restaurant, covered it with napkins, borrowed a pencil from one of the employees, and began their explanation. "On those napkins," he said, "we told the whole story. I drew three large circles representing the three degrees of glory, and we went from there. We told them about baptism, and they had lots of questions."

We all listened intently as this young man testified before the congregation of the truths he and his friend taught that night at McDonald's. "We were really pumped," he said. It was as though in answering the questions he discovered the strength of his own sure testimony. Indeed, these two young men were different. Through the baptismal covenant, they had committed to "stand as witnesses of God at all times and in all things, and in all places" (Mosiah 18:9). Yes, even at McDonald's. That night at McDonald's, two young men experienced the excitement and thrill of sharing something very precious with four young women who must have respected and trusted them and were now their friends, real friends.

It is important to have friends; a desire for friends is bone-marrow deep. Everyone wants to be liked. You can't have too many friends—real friends, that is. There are counterfeit friendships that go by the name of friends, but real friends are "allies of our better natures," always encouraging proper conduct and good times.

Sometimes the desire, the yearning—yes, the need—for friends can be so intense that people will be drawn to anyone just to fill that need. Counterfeit friendship can be very unwise and lead to much heartache. On the other hand, Latter-day Saint youth with sincere interest in and respect for people can gather many friends around them, both members and nonmembers. In the process they will watch out for each other, encourage each other, and help each other reach a higher purpose. Having a friend is important, and being a friend is equally important.

> Friends make the world more beautiful.
> They share their point of view
> And help us see things in a way
> That's wonderful and new.
> Friends make the world more beautiful
> In countless different ways,
> Making good times better
> And enriching all our days.
> (Authorship unknown)

As members of The Church of Jesus Christ of Latter-day Saints, we have not only the opportunity but the responsibility— not only the duty but the privilege—of becoming friends with everyone we meet. Learning how to be a friend with those who are not members of the Church can be a wonderful and rewarding experience. Becoming friends with members or nonmembers begins with what missionaries refer to as building relationships of trust. Do you think the four young women who called the two young men to teach them at McDonald's felt a relationship of trust? How does that happen, especially with nonmembers?

In the pamphlet *For the Strength of Youth,* the First Presidency speaks about friendshipping:

Everyone needs good friends. Your circle of friends will greatly influence your thinking and behavior, just as you will theirs. When you share common values with your friends, you can strengthen and encourage each other. If some of your friends are shy and do not feel included, be particularly sensitive to their feelings and go out of your way to pull them into the influence of your strong circle of good friends. Together you can maintain a high standard of gospel living.

Treat everyone with kindness and dignity. Invite your nonmember friends to Church activities where they can learn about your standards and the principles of the gospel. Include them in your midweek activities and your Sunday meetings. Help them feel welcome and wanted. Many nonmembers have come into the Church through friends who have involved them in Church activities. (P. 9.)

Recently I talked with Elder Moran from Virginia, who at the time was serving in the Canada Vancouver Mission. He joined the Church only one year before coming on his mission. I asked Elder Moran what experience he may have had with Latter-day Saint students in his school. He reported: "All the top students were Latter-day Saints. Out of a graduating class of six hundred, the top five who were valedictorians were all Mormons. I always thought they were doing something right, something that helped them stand out and achieve. They were good examples."

"Did you see them as being friendly?" I asked.

"They were all friendly, they were outgoing; I don't think there were any of them that weren't."

"What were some of the characteristics of the Mormons that you remember?"

"They were always happy when you would make eye contact with them. There was a friendly countenance about them, each and every one. You would see them talking with their friends, and they always looked like they were happy; they just seemed upbeat."

"Did they ever associate with you in groups where the standards were different?"

"Most of the time."

"How did you handle that?"

"My best friend who was a Latter-day Saint would get annoyed, especially if we took things too far or if things got out of hand. He would backlash us a little bit, tell us it wasn't proper. If the music we listened to wasn't appropriate, he excused himself from the situation, which to us was kind of weird, but we never made fun of him when he would leave."

"You didn't lose respect for him?"

"No, we would tease him about it, but he was still a good friend."

"Were you ever invited into the homes of your friends who were members of the Church?" I asked.

"Oh, yes."

"How was that?"

"That was interesting because my best friend's parents took time to talk to me. They talked about things we were interested in. We were involved in soccer, so that was something we usually talked about."

"Do you remember the first time you went to church as a nonmember, and do you remember how you felt?"

"Yes, I do. Wherever I was, church people would approach me and call me by name. I had a lot of attention, and it made me feel important. When you get that much attention you can't help but feel good."

It would be wonderful if all our friends were to become members of the Church and enjoy the blessings available, but this must not be our only reason for being friendly. Having friends is important to everyone. However, having friends is only half the relationship; being a friend is equally important. Good friends lift you, and when you are a good friend, you lift others. It has been said, "To have a friend, be a friend." Friends stick together; they encourage each other to do good. They do small acts of service for the sake of friendship, and sometimes they perform acts of sacrifice. Friends go out of their way for each other.

A group of young people on a bus trip from British Columbia to the Seattle Temple spoke freely about their many friends in schools where there are few Mormons. Linsey explained it this way: "To have nonmember friends, you have to be open to new ideas and be understanding. You have to want to be everyone's friend, respect others' beliefs, be a good listener, and be there for them. Immorality is the big issue, but I don't reject them when they choose differently. I try to help people know who they really are and respect themselves. I look at everyone as a child of God."

Tara joined in with a chuckle and explained, "At work one of the guys said to me, 'You're the kind of girl every guy wants to marry.' I asked, 'What do you mean?' He said, 'You haven't been around the block with everyone.' I said, 'I haven't even been around the corner.'" Good humor is a wonderful way to ease tension and build friendships.

Additional comments were freely expressed as the bus continued toward Seattle. "All my friends keep the standards. I just choose friends in and out of the Church who do," said Lanny.

Nathan added, "All my friends don't keep my standards, but I let them know right away what I'll do and won't do, and they respect that. They make sure I keep my own standards."

And Steven added, "My friends help me. If someone tries to get me to do something wrong, they help me."

Once again, Lanny spoke up. "A lot of my friends think it's cool that I have standards. They want to help me. I always try to be open and friendly and treat everybody the same. You have to have tolerance and respect people as they are." Nathan added an observation: "I've noticed kids who try to push their religion at school, but I try to teach by example. I've had friends who get into drugs and alcohol, and those friendships just end."

Thoughtfully, James told of a personal experience. "I had a nonmember girlfriend. We planned to marry, and then I told her

I could marry only someone who lived my standards. I had to tell her good-bye. It hurt a lot, and it still hurts. I don't think I'll date a nonmember again."

The pamphlet *For the Strength of Youth* also provides youth with a message from the First Presidency regarding dating. "Because dating is a preparation for marriage, date only those who have high standards, who respect your standards, and in whose company you can maintain the standards of the gospel of Jesus Christ" (p.7).

It is a natural desire to want to be popular, to want to be liked, to want to be with the in crowd, to want to be accepted and not rejected. Yet Elder Neal A. Maxwell provides wise counsel: "In so many respects, the world's ways head in opposite directions from gospel destinations. Because we are a covenant people, our behavioral loyalties are to be with the Lord." Elder Maxwell also quotes President N. Eldon Tanner, who cautioned, "This craving for praise and popularity too often controls actions, and as [people] succumb they find themselves bending their character when they think they are only taking a bow." Elder Maxwell continues, "Popularity can overwhelm the individual's inner sentinel or conscience, which stands guard over his soul by sounding inconvenient and uninvited alarms." ("Popularity and Principle," *Ensign,* March 1995, pp. 12, 13.)

Kent, a young man known for having many, many friends, is outgoing and athletic, plays the guitar, and speaks to everyone. He grew up in Vernon, British Columbia, as one of only a few members of the Church in his high school. I asked Kent, "How did you become friends with those who are not members of the church?"

In his outgoing, rather matter-of-fact way, he responded, "It's no challenge. You like people whether they are members or not, and you are drawn to them for the same reasons. The challenge is when you want to hide your candle under a bushel. If you are open and forthright about who you are and what you believe, the people you are drawn to and those who are drawn to you will be your friends. It is most unlikely that they will be drawn to you for some other reason than who you are. Any attempt to be other than who you are will limit a relationship. People like you for whatever reason. It's nothing magic. Being a friend with a nonmember, you just share with them what you would naturally share with a member friend."

"Kent," I asked, "can you think of a time when you had to tell a friend no and yet you didn't want to offend him or her?"

"Yes, all the time. They will test you to see if you are who you say you are. In high school we won a big basketball tournament, and one of the player's fathers hosted a party and provided alcohol. I went to the party. My teammate's younger brother started harassing me to have a glass of champagne. I refused three times, and then one of my teammates grabbed Larry and shook him and said, 'Bug off, he doesn't drink,' or words to that effect. Larry later on came and apologized and said he just wanted to see if I really didn't drink. That scenario has played itself out numerous times. In every instance except one, I have found that it has increased the esteem of the person who was offering the drink."

Rebecca, a returned missionary who served in Brazil, reflects on her high school days and her great desire for friends—girlfriends, boyfriends, member friends, nonmember friends, just friends, she said. "If I felt like a person didn't like me, it hurt my pride more than my heart. I didn't really 'love my neighbor,' I just wanted to be popular. Gratefully, that changed over the next few years. I became more interested in being a friend and liking people for who they are. I didn't win any popularity contests in high school, but I enjoyed many friendships with my nonmember peers, some of which were rich and rewarding.

"I remember when an enthusiastic missionary came to our early-morning seminary and shared with us his vision of how we could have nonmember friends. He set weekly after-school cottage meetings and challenged us to bring our friends for a Church film and informal discussions. Those cottage meetings were the starting place of some of my richest high school friend-ships. They provided an opportunity for us to discuss things that really mattered to us, much more than the plot of the latest movie or what went on at a recent party. I learned about the struggles my friends faced and came to care deeply about them, to pray for them, and to long for their happiness. Some of my friends actually took the missionary discussions. Only one joined the Church, but nonetheless my friendship with the others was deepened by the things we had shared, and I was blessed by their association."

Rebecca continued, "I believe there are a number of impor-tant skills in friendshipping, such as learning to listen, building on things we share in common, and making opportunities to do things together. But the big key, I believe, is simply to love. There will always be some who are offended by our differences and threatened by our love for them, but there will also be many who respond with their friendship. I've found that such relationships, whether or not they lead to a friend's conversion, are edifying and richly rewarding."

Young women who learn to make friends can be a great in-fluence in the lives of young men, whether members or non-members. Consider how one young woman befriended a young nonmember who is now serving a mission after only one year in the Church. A native of Seattle, Washington, who is proselyting in Spanish in the Canada Vancouver Mission, Elder Owens is serving as a district leader despite having been out relatively few months. Looking back, he says, "When I wasn't living the stan-dards the way I live them now, my Latter-day Saint friends didn't make me feel like I was an outcast. They could see I was not liv-ing their standards, but they let me know what their standards were and this helped me to easily fit into their environment. I at-tribute my conversion in part to their making it known to me what their standards were. By their acceptance of me I could be myself and still feel good around my nonmember friends."

"Were you ever invited into their homes?"

"Yes. They were a lot different from my home. I can recognize now that it was the Spirit that was there. The families were strong. All these little things made me think that there was something different about this entire group of people. The home was the most important thing to them. All the activities were centered around the home. Then there was this weird thing called family home evening. When I would invite my friend out on Monday night, he would always say, 'I can't.' And I would ask, 'Why not?' 'Because,' he would say, 'I have to be with my family.' I thought that was rather strange. I thought that was *really* strange."

"Did they ever invite you to family home evening, and were you ever there when they had family prayer?"

"Oh, yes. I was there one or two times. I had known about prayer before, but I had never thought about a family kneeling together and praying. All these things were strange to me. There was one family in particular that introduced me to all of this. I never knew that a family could be the center place for all activities, all learning. It was through this that I thought there was something more I could learn. I really enjoyed it."

"At what point did you become seriously interested in the Church?"

"Well, I had a friend who continually talked with me about the Church and the family and invited me over. I was really interested at the time. These people always had a light to them, a light of happiness. For me, I would be that way sometimes, but the rest of the time I was not happy. It wasn't a consistent thing."

"Was your friend a boy or a girl?"

"A girl. I have had numerous member friends who were boys, but they never approached me about the Church. I was really interested before. In fact, I lived only two blocks away from the church building. I lived there for two years and didn't even know what it was. I would see it filled on Sundays and weekday mornings, and kids would come out and I would think, *Why are they going into that place so early? It's not a school.* I was interested from the beginning. When she invited me over to her home for the first time, her whole family was friendly: her father, her mother, and her sisters. I ate dinner and felt like I was part of the family."

"What did she say to you when she invited you over? Did she give any explanation or anything?"

"Well, I learned that her parents had said to her, 'Why don't you invite Michael over for dinner.' So I went over. And then her dad told her to invite me over again, but this time they asked her, 'Why don't you invite him to listen to the missionaries?' She called and said, 'We have missionaries from our Church coming to our home. Would you be interested in coming over?' She told me later that she was really scared to ask me. I said, 'Do you have to wear a shirt and a tie and dress pants?' And she said, 'Yes.' I thought, *Oh, no.* I didn't wear that stuff, but when she asked me I said yes. I listened to the discussions, and here I am."

"Did you ever feel pressured, or were you ever offended by their anxiousness for your involvement?"

"Oh, no. I felt like they were on the sidelines cheering me on. It was just like my family in my activities and in my sports. It was more like they were expressing their joy and enthusiasm for what I was doing. Her parents were converts to the Church. They really helped me out. I didn't feel pushed at all."

"Elder Owens," I asked, "what would you say to a group of youth who want to become friends with nonmembers?"

"I would tell them that it is so important to always live your standards, always. For me, when I was around my member friends it was more of an escape, because when you're with your other friends there is a pressure. You're always thinking that you are going to have to do something that you know isn't right. I know that most youth know what's right and what's wrong, but when you're around friends who aren't members there is often a feeling of pressure to do something that isn't right. With my member friends, I felt free, free to just be a friend. I would say that the most important thing is to not get involved with the things the nonmember friends are doing if it goes against your standards. Provide an escape for them. Invite them to church activities. They will want to be around you because they will feel free and won't have any pressures."

"Did you ever think your member friends were just being friendly so you would join the Church?"

"I believe not, because the first thing they talked about with me was their families. I had many close Latter-day Saint friends because I trusted them. I didn't feel they were pushing me at all. I may have been turned off a bit if they had been pushy. There is a preparation that is necessary, just like the commitment pattern in missionary work. I didn't feel pressured; in fact, I was prepared. I could have been asked any time in the space of nine months and I would have said yes."

"What would you say to Latter-day Saint parents who may have some concern about their youth having nonmember friends?"

"I've heard parents say to use them as an excuse: 'If you need to, tell your friends your parents say you can't do it, if you are in a situation where you feel pressured to do something.' I'd say have faith in your kids. They are strong, and they know what's right, and if they see the example at home, they are going to do what's right. I'm going to have faith in my kids. When Latter-day Saint kids do the things they are supposed to be doing, they can take any kind of temptation and turn it into something good."

President Spencer W. Kimball said on one occasion, "The righteous woman's strength and influence today can be tenfold what it might be in more tranquil times" (*The Teachings of Spencer W. Kimball,* ed. Edward L. Kimball [Salt Lake City: Bookcraft, 1982], p. 326). Consider the righteous influence of the young woman who befriended Elder Owens by building a relationship of trust. Remember, "The worth of souls is great in the sight of God; . . . And if it so be that you should labor all your days in crying repentance unto this people, and bring, save it be one soul unto me, how great shall be your joy with him in the kingdom of my Father!" (D&C 18:10, 15.) How many souls will be brought into the kingdom of our Father because one young woman befriended a young man? It has been said that you can count the seeds in an apple, but you can't count the apples in a seed. And so it is in friendship.

Elder Russo, a native of California, had been in the Church only a year and two months when he came on his mission. I asked him, "If you were going to be talking to a group of Latter-day Saint youth, and you were asked the question, 'How can we become friends with nonmembers?' what would you say?"

"Show them that you care and that you are going to be there for them. Sometimes Latter-day Saint kids are hard on nonmembers and drive them away. Just keep the Church standards in everyday life, and it shines right through. More important than what you say is how you live."

Maria Burnham is a thirteen-year-old member and the youngest of eleven children. She has watched her older brothers and sisters befriend members and nonmembers for years. She has learned how to make friends. "Maria," I questioned, "how do you handle it when your nonmember friends invite you to do things you shouldn't?"

"I just ignore them when they want me to do something wrong. The kids aren't bad even though their standards may be different, so it's not difficult to make friends. I've been in challenging situations lots of times, and I just go and do something else; there is always something else to do. I just don't want to feel bad afterwards about anything I may do. If you're worrying about someone finding out about something you've done, it ruins your life."

Writer Chris Crowe offers some great ideas for making friends:

Be a good influence on others. When I was a sophomore in high school, some of my friends started drinking and smoking. They knew I didn't drink or smoke, but they began to pressure me to join their parties anyway. The more they pressured me, the more uncomfortable I felt, until finally I stopped hanging around them. I figured that if they were really my friends, they wouldn't push me to do things I didn't want to do. Real friends would never ask you to do something you shouldn't.

Really, this friendly advice is basically what you'd do if you followed the Savior's advice to 'love one another.' If you really work at loving those around you, and show that love, you'll be the kind of friend everybody wants. ("Some Friendly Advice," *New Era,* March 1995, p. 11.)

Shelly was not quite sixteen when a young man invited her to a school dance. It's hard to hold the standard sometimes, especially when it seems that all your friends are going. Shelly tried to explain the standard of not dating until you're sixteen. "It was really hard," she said, "especially when you don't understand yourself that even though you are almost sixteen, you have to wait. Sometimes it just doesn't make sense. I guess it's just a matter of obedience. After struggling to say no when I wanted to say yes, I felt terrible. It hurt, until my friend who had invited me left the following note in my locker: "Hi, Shelly. I think you're great. Through all the times I have been privileged to be with you, I have never failed to be impressed. You are one of the very few people who live exactly the way they profess to live. That is unique, an exceptional accomplishment. You have so many gifts and have learned to use them wisely. Your spirit is full of life and giving. You are so willing to share. You bless all who know you; no wonder so many people watch and follow your example. God bless you, Shelly." Shelly survived that hard time, and the following year she had many dates and many friends, both members and nonmembers.

Years ago when I had just turned sixteen, I left my small hometown of Glenwood, Alberta, Canada, which has a population of approximately three hundred people. I went away for my senior year of high school because the courses I needed for graduation were not available to me at home. I knew only one person in my new school, and I was scared. I hadn't had any experience in making friends except with those kids I had grown up with. I didn't wear the latest fashions like the other girls, so I looked different. I wasn't a part of the in group or of any group, for that matter. I was away from home, homesick, and lonesome. Even if they had asked me, I didn't have the money to do the things the other kids did. I yearned for friends. There was so much talking going on, it seemed that everyone else had lots of friends. *How do you get in?* I wondered. No one was discourteous, but I felt ignored, as if they didn't know I was there.

Can you imagine how desperately I wanted friends, or at least one friend? I remember feeling alone, a long way from home. Kneeling by my bed day after day, night and morning, I prayed for friends, I pleaded for friends. I wanted boyfriends, girlfriends, young and older friends, member and nonmember friends. I felt I needed friends for my survival. I talked to my Father in Heaven and promised that in every way I would strive to do what was right no matter what, if I could just be helped to know how to make friends in my new situation. The thought came to my mind that maybe there were others who felt like I did; maybe I should try to forget about myself and be a friend first. I thought, *I can smile, and I can say hi.*

I believe that thought was a whispering of the Spirit in answer to my prayer. I began to focus on being a friend instead of having a friend. I listened to the Spirit. I did smile, and I said hi to everyone. I learned to be friendly. At first it was hard, but before long it became easier. At the end of my senior year, I was nominated by the student body as the representative girl for the high school where I had attended only one year. Some may have considered it a popularity victory, but I'll always know it was in answer to the fervent prayer of a sixteen-year-old who learned how to be friends with everybody.

To be friends with those who are not members of the Church,

you can enrich a life and maybe even save a life. In the song "Be That Friend" by Michael McLean, we learn of the blessing of friendship:

> Well, your friends know what's right,
> And your friends know what's wrong,
> And your friends all know sometimes it hard to choose.
> But the friend who helps you see
> Where the choices will lead,
> Is the kind of friend you never want to lose.

We have the perfect example in our Lord and Savior, Jesus Christ. He loved and served everyone and said to all of us, "A new commandment I give unto you, That ye love one another; as I have loved you, that ye also love one another. By this shall all men know that ye are my disciples, if ye have love one to another." (John 13:34–35.)

Ardeth Kapp has been an elementary school teacher, a college instructor, and the writer and instructor for a television series. A former Young Women general president, she served with her husband, Heber B. Kapp, when he presided over the Canada Vancouver Mission.

10

BEING FRIENDS WITH CHURCH LEADERS

Jack R. Christianson

While walking to a lecture through a busy hallway at Brigham Young University one day, I passed a woman who looked very familiar to me. After making eye contact, she said, "Hello, Bishop. How have you been?" I warmly said hello. I knew I knew her, but it didn't click. After a few words and a few seconds, my memory began to work and I remembered that she had been a member of a ward where I served as bishop some ten years before. As she briefly told me about her husband and three children, I began to remember that she had really struggled with some of the counsel I had given her while she attended our ward at BYU. I couldn't remember any details, but she reminded me that she hadn't cared too much for me. She had thought I was far too strict and used far too many scriptures when I spoke to the ward. It was nice to see her, but I felt a little bad that her memories of me as her student ward bishop were somewhat negative.

She asked if I was speaking at the conference all week. I informed her that I was and invited her, if she had time, to attend one or all of my lectures. She said she might come. I then expressed how wonderful it was to see her and how grateful I was that she still remembered me. I went to my lecture without giving the encounter a great deal of further thought, because the necessity of remembering my talk was pressing on my mind.

The next day I noticed her in one of my presentations. She attended the following day also, and the next. After the final talk, while I was shaking hands with people, I noticed her standing in line crying. I thought, *Oh no! I've offended her again.* When she shook my hand, she begged me to forgive her for the negative feelings she had felt for so long and then said, "Boy, Bishop, you sure have changed! I can't believe how different you are now than you were ten years ago."

She then expressed how much she had enjoyed the lectures and how much she had learned. I thanked her, and I then nearly bit my tongue trying not to say, "Well, Sister, it's almost the same stuff I tried to give you ten years ago when you thought I was so strict." Of course, I didn't say anything at the time. But as I drove home that evening, I thought, *Sure I've changed some, but she's the one who has changed!* She had been married in the temple, given birth to three children, and experienced an entire decade of life and growth since she was a freshman in college. She now viewed her former Church leader in an entirely different light. She thought it was him who had changed. With time, she had matured to the point where she could understand and see more clearly. The Spirit of the Lord was operating in her life, allowing her to see things as they "really are" and as they "really will be" (Jacob 4:13).

She was viewing life with different eyes. She had finally realized that her bishop was her advocate and friend, not someone who was trying to control her life or always tell her what to do. The bishop had become a real, touchable human being.

Sometimes when we are young, it is easy to view our Church

leaders as people who are so far removed from where we are that they seem unapproachable. At times, it appears that they are to be feared because they know our parents (or *are* our parents) and that they just don't understand us. When these feelings arise, we must try to remember that the Lord called them. Sure, they are not perfect. They do have weaknesses. They are human beings going through many of the same trials you are going through. They are mortals, and yes, because of that they do make mistakes at times. However, can we give them the benefit of the doubt most of the time? They have been called to represent the Lord to us; however, they have not been called to represent us to the Lord. They are people, real people who are just a little further along the path of life than you. But because they have sacred callings, they are different. They are our leaders but also our friends. They really can understand us!

Jesus taught us that the greatest among us "shall be servant of all" (Mark 10:44). He came not to be served but to serve! (See Mark 10:45.) He was and is the greatest Church leader of all, and he came to serve us. He even called us his friends if we will just do what he has asked us to do: "This is my commandment, That ye love one another, as I have loved you. Greater love hath no man than this, that a man lay down his life for his friends. Ye are my friends, if ye do whatsoever I command you. Henceforth I call you not servants; for the servant knoweth not what his lord doeth: but I have called you friends; for all things that I have heard of my Father I have made known unto you." (John 15: 12–15.)

Just as my former student ward member changed when she saw me as a human being who loved her rather than as a harsh, strict ruler, so we can change as we begin to be friends with our Church leaders and begin to trust them as we would our dearest friends. Perhaps that trust may be violated from time to time, but in most cases you can trust your Church leaders, particularly your bishops and stake presidents, with any of your deepest concerns, questions, doubts, and fears. Remember, we love Christ so much "because he first loved us" (1 John 4:19).

We can love our leaders, because in most cases they loved us first—even when we feel guilty, worthless, dirty, and ashamed. They not only love you, but they can understand you. They have been through much of what you are going through.

I remember when I was a young bishop many years ago that a dear young sister came to me to confess some very serious sins. Some of her first words were, "Bishop, I know you won't be able to understand because you're so perfect and you've never done anything wrong in your life!" I almost laughed, but I didn't. She thought that because I was the bishop, I must be perfect. I assured her that I wasn't, and I asked her to go ahead and tell me and see if I just might understand a little bit how she felt. I don't remember exactly how it turned out, but I do remember having a spiritual talk as we discussed the Savior and his atonement.

Alma taught why Christ can understand us and love us no matter what we have done:

> And he shall go forth, suffering pains and afflictions and temptations of every kind; and this that the word might be fulfilled which saith he will take upon him the pains and the sicknesses of his people.
>
> And he will take upon him death, that he may loose the bands of death which bind his people; and he will take upon him their infirmities, that his bowels may be filled with mercy, according to the flesh, that he may know according to the flesh how to succor his people according to their infirmities. (Alma 7:11–12.)

As the Lord's representatives, our Church leaders can also understand us because most of them have his Spirit with them. As common judges in Israel, they have been given the gift of discernment if they strive to live close to the Spirit. This is another reason why we need not fear them. This is also why it makes such a difference for you and me to have the Spirit ourselves, so that we can look beyond their inadequacies and mortal weaknesses and view them as servants of God. We must understand that, regardless of what we think or feel about our Church leaders personally, they were called by the Lord to lead us. The Prophet Joseph Smith taught: "Every man who has a calling to minister to the inhabitants of the world was ordained to that very purpose in the Grand Council of heaven before this world was. I suppose I was ordained to this very office in that Grand Council." (*Teachings of the Prophet Joseph Smith,* comp. Joseph Fielding Smith [Salt Lake City: Deseret Book Co., 1977], p. 365.)

Remember, as President Gordon B. Hinckley has so eloquently taught, this church belongs to Christ, the Son of God, not to the members or to any of its leaders. We are all in this thing together. President Hinckley said:

> This church does not belong to its President. Its head is the Lord Jesus Christ, whose name each of us has taken upon ourselves. We are all in this great endeavor together. We are here to assist our Father in His work and His glory, "to bring to pass the immortality and eternal life of man" (Moses 1:39). Your obligation is as serious in your sphere of responsibility as is my obligation in my sphere. No calling in this church is small or of little consequence. All of us in the pursuit of our duty touch the lives of others. To each of us in our respective responsibilities the Lord has said: "Wherefore, be faithful; stand in the office which I have appointed unto you; succor the weak, lift up the hands which hang down, and strengthen the feeble knees" (D&C 81:5). ("This Is the Work of the Master," *Ensign,* May 1995, p. 71.)

We must be friends with our Church leaders so we can help our Father in his work and his glory. Again, we must be unified and be one, or we cannot be his (see D&C 38:27).

I have served as a Church leader in many capacities. Currently I am serving as a bishop for the second time. Nothing is more rewarding than having a close relationship and friendship with our youth. I love them beyond words. But because I love them so deeply, I interview them regularly and thoroughly. I ask

every question in every interview. I never assume that everything
is always in order. It has nothing to do with me not trusting the
youth, but as the Lord's representative I need to love them
enough to help them in any way that I can to have the Spirit and
to keep their covenants. I have found that when we trust each
other and have open dialogue, great things can happen.

I always let people know three things about our interviews.
First, everything we talk about is strictly confidential, and it will
never be shared with any other human being without the individual's permission. Second, I would never think less of them no
matter what they may confess or tell me. Third, I probably won't
remember in the future most of what we talk about without
some major jogging of my memory. After things are taken care
of, I try to eliminate them from my mind. I try to do what the
Lord does when a person repents: "Behold, he who has repented
of his sins, the same is forgiven, and I, the Lord, remember them
no more" (D&C 58:42).

Elder Jeffrey R. Holland of the Quorum of the Twelve
Apostles has talked about why Church leaders care so much for
the youth they serve:

> Believe it or not we, too, were young once, though I know that
> strains the very limits of your imagination. Equally unfathomable
> is the fact that your parents were once young also, and so were
> your bishops and your quorum advisers. But as the years have
> gone by we have learned many lessons beyond those of youth—
> that, for example, Noah's wife was *not* named Joan of Arc, and, so
> far as we know, Pontius Pilate flew no commercial aircraft of any
> kind. Why do you think we now try so hard and worry so much
> and want the very best for you? It is because we have been your
> age and you have never been ours, and we have learned some
> things you do not yet know.
>
> When you are young not all of life's questions and difficulties
> have arisen yet, but they will arise, and, unfortunately for your
> generation, they will arise at a younger and younger age. The
> gospel of Jesus Christ marks the only sure and safe path. So older

men, seasoned men—men passing on to you the legacy of history—continue to call out to youth. ["Our Priesthood Legacy," *Ensign,* May 1995, p. 38.]

Our leaders were once young people themselves! We want you "to be more wise than we have been" (Mormon 9:31). This concept was taught to me by a bishop who, as the years progressed, became one of my dearest and closest friends. In fact, just a short time before writing this chapter I had the privilege of speaking at his funeral. We had become such good friends that when he knew his condition was terminal, he came to my home and asked me to perform that honor. Since his death, two stories that I am about to share have become more dear to me than ever before. I have pondered, laughed, and cried over them. These experiences changed in a dramatic fashion the way I look at and view all my Church leaders. I knew my leader wasn't perfect, but I also knew that I wasn't! I wanted to be friends with this man because I knew he was the Lord's representative for me.

The first experience took place on one of the first fast Sundays I was home from my mission. Our bishopric had changed while I was serving, and the man who had become bishop was unfamiliar to me. I don't remember him living in the ward before I left, but I felt like I knew him by the time I returned home because he had written me several letters. He also had interviewed me very carefully when I returned and had made an effort to be friendly with me whenever I saw him. Almost instantly a bond between us was formed. I began to love and trust him deeply. He called me to be the priest quorum adviser and Explorer leader, so we worked very closely together right from the beginning.

Anyway, we had just finished fast and testimony meeting and were leaving the chapel for home. Bishop Thomas was standing at the doorway shaking hands with everyone as they were leaving. He was a short, plump man with a bald head and glasses. His smile and spirit were disarming. As he shook my hand, he asked, "Well, Elder, how did you enjoy your first testimony meeting here in the old ward?"

I responded by telling him that it was great to be home, but I wished people would learn to bear pure testimonies and quit giving travelogues about their families. I didn't realize then how much of a Pharisee I had become and how judgmental I was being.

Bishop Thomas gently took me by the arm and led me to a corner of the room behind a propped-open wooden door. He then said, "You know, Elder, there is only one judge in this ward, and it's me!" He then very calmly walked away and went back to shaking hands with the people. I was stunned, needless to say. I stood there looking like a puppy that had just received a whipping. His words sank deep into my heart.

Now, the lesson. I never even thought about being offended. I knew he loved me, and, with more thought on the matter, I realized how right he was. He loved me enough to be firm with me when necessary but gentle enough to teach me rather than preach to me! With time and a more mature perspective, I have learned that he had been as the prophet Lehi taught: a "true friend . . . forever" (2 Nephi 1:30). He was a man of steel and velvet. He loved me enough to do what was right, not what was easy.

I can't remember if I ever shared with him the lesson I learned that day. I learned that in each ward, there is but one person who has the right to pass judgment on others: the bishop. In a stake, the stake president also acts as a common judge in Israel. On a general level, all the General Authorities are judges. The rest of the Church doesn't need to carry the burden of judging anyone, not even themselves! We all have a judge with whom we can meet who represents the Lord. He has been given the authority to pass judgment on our worthiness, and no one else has that right!

In my service as a bishop, this lesson has been one of the most meaningful I've learned in my life. The Lord and his servants can judge people and situations, and unless I'm one of the ordained servants, I just have to worry about keeping myself where I need to be and about those I have stewardship over.

I learned that I need my leaders and that I need to do all I can to be friends with them because, as the Savior taught, "What I the Lord have spoken, I have spoken, and I excuse not myself; and though the heavens and the earth pass away, my word shall not pass away, but shall all be fulfilled, whether by mine own voice or by the voice of my servants, it is the same" (D&C 1:38).

My second experience with Bishop Thomas happened when he and I took all our priests on a hike up Mount Nebo near Nephi, Utah. It was a grueling hike because it took much of the day to get to the spot where we would spend the night. Our plan was to have a devotional around the campfire and then have a testimony meeting. The following morning we would climb to the summit, which is nearly twelve thousand feet above sea level, and watch the sunrise, have another devotional, and then hike all the way back down.

Everything went as planned except that one of our young men became deathly ill and began vomiting at about 9:00 P.M., during the testimony meeting. His sleeping bag was now wet and stinky, so I volunteered to give him mine for the night. I was sure I could keep warm by lying next to the fire with a small blanket—after all, it was August. However, at that high altitude by midnight it was freezing! I tried to keep warm, but it was useless. I thought everyone was asleep, so I determined just to tough it out for a few hours. However, Bishop Thomas was not asleep. After watching me struggle for a few minutes, he finally asked jokingly, "Are you a little cold, Jackie boy?"

I laughed with him and said, "Oh, I'll be all right. It's just a bit nippy, that's all."

He laughed and then insisted that I come and get into his sleeping bag with him. I thought that would be uncomfortable, so I told him again that it was okay and that I'd be all right.

Again, he insisted. So I obeyed my bishop and wiggled my way into his bag. The only problem was that I weighed two hundred pounds and he, as I mentioned, was quite a plump little fellow.

We talked and laughed until our sides ached. Sleep was gone from both of us. It was totally uncomfortable but very warm.

After we stopped laughing, one of the great learning experiences of my life began. Bishop Thomas told me the deepest feelings of his heart. He shared with me his fears, his testimony, his love for the Lord and his family. We both cried at times. We looked at the stars together and discussed the eternities. We listened to the wind whisper through the trees and the coyotes howl across the canyons to each other. He committed me to keep my covenants, and he told me that I needed to be a teacher, not a lawyer.

I remember how I felt. I had wanted to be a lawyer for years. But now, after this sacred night, I wasn't sure what I should do. Of course, in the end I became a teacher and have loved almost every day of it.

That sacred night that changed the course of my life finally came to an end. As I sat at the summit of Mount Nebo the following morning watching the sun's rays break across the mountaintops, I knew I had participated in a once-in-a-lifetime experience. Words seem inadequate to express how I learned to love and trust my leaders after that night in Bishop Thomas's sleeping bag. I had made an eternal friend forever!

As I told both of these stories at Bishop Thomas's funeral, the tears came easily. I loved him. I still love him! I only pray that somehow I can be a friend to the people in our ward as he was to me.

Remember the young student ward member in the story at the beginning of this chapter? Remember that she said she thought I had changed so much? Well, maybe I had. We all change when we are friends with our Church leaders. Our fear of them flees because we love them and they love us. We know they are called of God, and therefore we learn to trust them. We strive to have the Spirit so that we can see clearly and not be on the outside.

As we strive to be friends with our Church leaders, let us ponder the words and love of our leader, President Gordon B. Hinckley. Speaking of his role as our leader, he expressed:

> I love the people of this church, of all ages, of all races, and of many nations.
>
> I love the children. They are very much the same the world over. Regardless of the color of their skin and of the circumstances in which they live, they carry with them a beauty that comes of innocence and of the fact that it was not long ago that they lived with their Father in Heaven. How lovely you are, wherever you are, you precious children.
>
> I love the youth of the Church. I have said again and again that I think we have never had a better generation than this. How grateful I am for your integrity, for your ambition to train your minds and your hands to do good work, for your love for the word of the Lord, and for your desire to walk in paths of virtue and truth and goodness.
>
> . . . Now, my brethren and sisters, the time has come for us to stand a little taller, to lift our eyes and stretch our minds to a greater comprehension and understanding of the grand millennial mission of this The Church of Jesus Christ of Latter-day Saints. This is a season to be strong. It is a time to move forward without hesitation, knowing well the meaning, the breadth, and the importance of our mission. It is a time to do what is right regardless of the consequences that might follow. It is a time to be found keeping the commandments. It is a season to reach out with kindness and love to those in distress and to those who are wandering in darkness and pain. It is a time to be considerate and good, decent and courteous toward one another in all of our relationships. In other words, to become more Christlike. ("This Is the Work of the Master," *Ensign*, May 1995, pp. 70, 71.)

If we can "stand a little taller" and understand our mission as members of Christ's true church a little better and be more

Christlike in all our relationships, we will have learned how to be friends with our Church leaders. We will become a Zion people, and the Lord will be able to say of us as he did of the people of Enoch: "And the Lord called his people Zion, because they were of one heart and one mind, and dwelt in righteousness; and there was no poor among them" (Moses 7:18).

Jack R. Christianson has taught in the Church Educational System for many years and currently teaches at the Orem, Utah, Institute of Religion. He is a popular speaker and is the author of several books and tapes. He and his wife, Melanie, are the parents of four daughters.

11

BEING FRIENDS WITH YOUR ANCESTORS

Wendy Bradford Wright

When I was in the eighth grade, our English teacher, Mr. Duncan, introduced the class to the fascinating subject of family history. Through his assignment, I became acquainted with several of my ancestors, some of whom gave up much for religious freedom. My twelfth great-grandfather, William Bradford, became the governor of Plymouth colony after making the journey across the Atlantic on the *Mayflower*. At least two of his descendants became Methodist ministers, the same faith my parents chose to follow. Consequently I had been raised in a good churchgoing home, but we lacked the truths that bring full understanding.

During my teens, I had the opportunity to hear the gospel message, first from Latter-day Saint friends and then from the missionaries. During the missionary discussions, the concept that immediately caught my attention was that of eternal families. Was it really possible to again see my ancestors whom I'd grown to admire so much and my grandfathers who had died when I was young?

I began to soak up the gospel truths taught to me. I was baptized, and soon after I received my patriarchal blessing. I was told that I had come to earth through a noble lineage and that I should seek out my kindred dead. From these inspired words, I began to realize how important family history would become in my life. One of the phrases in my blessing stated, "You will be a Savior on Mount Zion for relatives who have gone on before you." I believed the words of the Prophet Joseph Smith: "The greatest responsibility in this world that God has laid upon us is to seek after our dead" (*Teachings of the Prophet Joseph Smith,* comp. Joseph Fielding Smith [Salt Lake City: Deseret Book Co., 1977], p. 356). He also said that "those Saints who neglect it . . . do it at the peril of their own salvation" (ibid., p. 193).

Before I was married, I gathered the bits of information that my parents had obtained from other relatives. I planned to jump right into searching for ancestors further back on our pedigree, but as is so often the case my time got filled with other things, some important, some trivial. My ancestors were set on the shelf as I attended college and became engrossed in homemaking and impending motherhood.

Sometimes, though, our anxious ancestors are allowed to give us a swift kick to bring us back to the important matters of life. One night as I slept, I had a dream so real that to this day I can remember vivid details. My husband, Randal, and I were living in a small basement apartment in Provo, Utah, while we attended Brigham Young University. During the night, I suddenly awoke. I opened the bedroom door and, to my utter delight, found my Grandpa Bradford sitting on the old, ugly turquoise couch in our living room.

I had been thirteen when Grandpa died. We had been very close friends, and I admired and loved him greatly. His passing left a huge void in my life, one that seemed to get bigger instead of diminishing over time. Whenever I thought about Grandpa, I'd envision him floating in complete darkness with a sad look on his face. An intense fear of death enveloped me after his passing. I had never attended a funeral or seen a person who had passed away, and the thought of doing so brought a dread that was sometimes hard to shake. Even though my fears should have been squelched by the understanding I had gained from gospel principles, such as life after death and the resurrection, these fears were deeply imbedded and it was hard to fully grasp that these truths applied to me and my family.

Until I found my grandfather sitting on our couch! My previous fear of death was not present at all. It didn't seem strange to have Grandpa sitting there looking up at me. I wanted to run and throw my arms around him. I had missed him so much! But the look on his face made me stop quickly. It was apparent that he had been allowed to come for a specific reason. As I studied his face, I noticed that same sad look that had plagued my thoughts and dreams of the past.

Grandpa looked straight into my eyes and asked, "Why haven't you done my temple work?" I stood dumbfounded with a deep sense of guilt flowing over me, unable to reply. Again he asked: "Wendy, why haven't you done my temple work? Don't you realize that there are many, many people depending on you? You are the only person in the family who can help us!" The full impact of my responsibility as the only member of the Church in my family hit me, and I finally said, "I will, Grandpa, I will!"

The next morning I awoke feeling wonder about the event that had taken place the night before. I knew for a certainty that my grandfather had accepted the gospel truths in the spirit world, but he was unable to receive the needed ordinances there. A great desire welled up inside me to gather the necessary information so the saving ordinances could be performed for him and other relatives who were waiting. Joseph Fielding Smith said concerning the dead: "Thousands of men and women have died without knowing of Jesus Christ, or having an understanding of the nature of the laws of God; . . . All of these people are under the necessity of repentance and the Gospel will be taught to them in the world of spirits in its fulness. If they accept it there will be given to them the right of the essential ordinances administered vicariously in the Temples of the Lord, and they will become heirs in the celestial kingdom." (*Church History and Modern Revelation* [Melchizedek Priesthood study manual, 1949], pp. 136–37.)

When my husband and I walked into the baptistry at the Provo Temple a few weeks later, we immediately sensed an immense feeling of anticipation and joy. We knew that Grandpa was near and that the joy we felt was radiating from him and his sincere desire to be baptized. Randal was lowered into the waters of the baptismal font as Grandpa's proxy. We again experienced this happy feeling during the endowment session and later when Grandpa was sealed by proxy to his parents, along with his brothers and sisters.

Since that time, I have conducted much research for these family members of the past. Not only have the necessary names, dates, and places been found, but actual historical and biographical information has been gathered, making these people even more real and special to me. They have become my friends. As Elder W. Grant Bangerter reminds us: "May we always remember that we perform the temple ordinances for people and not for names. Those we call 'the dead' are alive in the spirit and are present in the temple." ("What Temples Are For," *Ensign,* May 1982, p. 72.) Our family, including most of our children, have been able to perform the baptisms, endowments, and sealings for my relatives, forming the eternal family units that I longed to have from the beginning of my Church membership. We feel a strong bond and friendship with our ancestors and will rejoice when we meet together again.

Many of you may think that family history is only for people like me who don't have Latter-day Saint relatives or that this duty is only for older people. But we can all become friends with our ancestors. Here are some ways:

Talk about the good old days. Invite your grandparents or other older relatives into your home to tell what it was like in their early years. Encourage them to tell interesting events that happened in their lives and some of the changes that have occurred in the world since they were young. If at all possible, tape-record their words.

Visit a stake or ward family history center. Have the consultants help you look for your family names on the I.G.I. (International Genealogical Index), where millions of names have been compiled as temple work for these people has been performed. Doing this will help you know which of your relatives still need temple work done. Prepare the needed information for those who need these saving ordinances, then plan a time that your family can make a trip to the temple.

Hold an ancestor night. For family home evening one night, study journals, stories, pictures, and other records that tell you something about your ancestors. Perhaps you could also prepare a meal from their native country.

Prepare an ancestor scrapbook. Build a picture pedigree of as many people as possible, striving to reach as far back into history as you can. Also consider including any newspaper clippings, other pictures, or any other items of interest you have in your possession. Some have even written original poetry about ancestors to include.

Elder J. Richard Clarke shares his feelings about friendshipping our ancestors: "Through family history we discover the most beautiful tree in the forest of creation—our family tree. Its numerous roots reach back through history, and its branches extend throughout eternity. Family history is the expansive expression of eternal love. It is born of selflessness. It provides opportunity to secure the family unit forever." ("Our Kindred Family—Expression of Eternal Love," *Ensign*, May 1989, p. 60.)

We all need to take an active role in this friendshipping process. My Grandma Freeman passed away recently at ninety years of age. She was one of the most special people in my life. I will always remember her fine example. Our family is looking forward to completing her work in the Dallas temple next year. Nichelle, our almost-twelve-year-old, will have the opportunity of being baptized in behalf of her great-grandmother. Although she has not known her as well as our older children have, she will feel very close to her grandma as she helps bring our family circle closer.

It is so important to become friends with our ancestors! As the Lord tells us, they are our link to happiness in the hereafter: "They without us cannot be made perfect—neither can we without our dead be made perfect" (D&C 128:15). It has been said that our ancestors will fall down at our feet and thank us for performing those ordinances in the temple that they cannot do themselves.

With this in mind, let us participate in the research process, the digging and the praying necessary to bring our ancestors into the full eternal families we need and want. President Spencer W. Kimball helped put our duties of seeking after our dead into the proper time frame: "I feel the same sense of urgency about temple work for the dead as I do about the missionary work for the living, since they are basically one and the same. . . . This work for the dead is constantly on my mind." ("The True Way of Life and Salvation," *Ensign,* May 1978, p. 4.) May we also have the work for our friends from the past constantly on our minds.

Wendy Bradford Wright *earned her bachelor's degree in family history from Brigham Young University and is an accredited genealogist. She is a part-time institute instructor and serves in her ward's Young Women presidency. She and her husband, Randal, have five children.*

12

BEING FRIENDS WITH PAST AND PRESENT PROPHETS

Todd Parker

R ick, please turn this car around and take me to work!" Such was my plea to a friend who had volunteered to give me a ride to my work at a cafeteria—but he was driving the wrong direction. "Look for my grandfather's truck. I just need to talk to him for a minute," was the reply as we sped up Ogden Canyon toward Pineview Reservoir. In reality Rick was stalling for time in order to get me to a campground where a surprise birthday party and a surprise guest from out of state awaited me. All I knew was my present situation: that I needed to be to work by noon to wash dishes, scrub floors, and clean tables for $1.25 per hour. Rick, however, knew my future prospects: hot dogs, marshmallows, friends, gifts—and that my friend's cousin had volunteered to work my shift so I could be the guest of honor at the party.

So it is with life. Many teenagers see only the present, getting caught up in the world of friends, school, sports, homework, daily routine, and television. Our prophets, who see the future, preach and teach about future blessings that await those who live faithful lives. Just as I didn't want to follow my friend Rick because what he was telling me didn't seem relevant to me, sometimes youth don't want to follow the counsel of older gentlemen called "the Brethren," since what they say doesn't seem to be relevant to them at the time. However, a failure to heed those who have insight to the future can lead not only to disappointment but also to a forfeiture of great joy and happiness.

Hopefully this chapter will help youth prevent themselves from missing the wonderful blessings that await when they listen to their friends the prophets, seers, and revelators of the Church. The Lord will never allow the prophets to lead his friends astray. The Lord told Moses, "But the prophet, which shall presume to speak a word in my name, which I have not commanded him to speak, . . . even that prophet shall die" (Deuteronomy 18:20).

President Harold B. Lee echoed this same truth when he observed: "We have a mouthpiece to whom God is revealing his mind and will. God will never permit him to lead us astray. As has been said, God would remove us out of our place if we should attempt to do it." (*Charge to Religious Educators,* 2nd ed. [Salt Lake City: Church of Jesus Christ of Latter-day Saints, 1981], p. 112.)

Becoming friends with prophets, becoming acquainted with and obedient to their teachings, will help insure your future safety and happiness. A true friend will always protect you, want what is best for you, and help you become the best you can be. So it is with prophets, both past and present. They want you to succeed, and the Lord will not allow them to give you incorrect counsel. The Lord taught, "He that receiveth a prophet in the name of a prophet shall receive a prophet's reward" (Matthew 10:41). Listening to the Lord's anointed and heeding their counsel brings great rewards.

One may ask, If we have a modern prophet, why are we told

to constantly study scriptures written by past prophets? Joseph Smith taught, "We never inquire at the hand of God for special revelation only in case of there being no previous revelation to suit the case" (*Teachings of the Prophet Joseph Smith,* comp. Joseph Fielding Smith [Salt Lake City: Deseret Book Co., 1977], p. 22). The Lord does not constantly rereveal his truths to his children through his mouthpiece the prophet. The Lord expects us to search out truths for ourselves through the words of the past prophets. This process is not only good for us but necessary for our growth.

Worldly Wisdom vs. Prophetic Warnings

One of the ways the prophets act as our friends is to help us keep an eternal perspective in a temporal and telestial world. The world entices us in one direction while the prophets exhort us in another direction. This conflict is illustrated in Lehi's dream. The prophet Lehi told his family to hold to the rod of iron, or the word of God as given through prophets (see 1 Nephi 11:25). The great and spacious building represented the world and the pride and wisdom thereof (see 1 Nephi 11:35–36). Things are not so different today. Often what the world encourages is in direct opposition to what the prophets teach.

For example, President Ezra Taft Benson's teaching concerning changing human nature is in direct opposition to the worldview held by many. "The Lord works from the inside out. The world works from the outside in. The world would take people out of the slums. Christ takes the slums out of the people, and then they take themselves out of the slums. The world would mold men by changing their environment. Christ changes men, who then change their environment. The world would shape human behavior, but Christ can change human nature." (*A Witness and a Warning* [Salt Lake City: Deseret Book Co., 1988], p. 64.)

President Benson has encouraged us to use the teachings of past prophets as contained in the Book of Mormon to combat false philosophies commonly taught today. Like Lehi, he gave us a challenge to turn away from the great and spacious building, or the world and the wisdom thereof: "Now, we have not been using the Book of Mormon as we should. Our homes are not as strong unless we are using it to bring our children to Christ. Our families may be corrupted by worldly trends and teachings unless we know how to use the book to expose and combat the falsehoods in socialism, organic evolution, rationalism, humanism, and so forth." (Ibid., p. 6.)

Those inside the great and spacious building exemplify people to whom wealth and popularity are of first importance (see 1 Nephi 8:27–28). President Benson has given a latter-day warning to people who would be thus tempted: *The two groups who have the greatest difficulty in following the prophet are the proud who are learned and the proud who are rich.* The learned may feel the prophet is only inspired when he agrees with them; otherwise, the prophet is just giving his opinion—speaking as a man. The rich may feel they have no need to take counsel of a lowly prophet." ("Fourteen Fundamentals in Following the Prophet," *1980 Devotional Speeches of the Year,* [Provo, Utah: Brigham Young University Press, 1981], p. 29.)

The world often gauges success in terms of wealth, possessions, or income. Magazines and news reports often list the most successful men, women, and businesses based on the amount of profit they accrue in one year. Students choosing careers meet with counselors who provide information on employment and salaries. Colleges and universities list salary scales to help future graduates choose a profession. Sadly, many people are often labeled or judged by how much money they make. Contrary to what the world would say, Brigham Young stated: "The worst fear I have about this people is that they will get rich in this country, forget God and His people, wax fat, and kick themselves out of the Church and go to hell. This people will stand mobbing, robbing, poverty, and all manner of persecution, and be true. But my greater fear . . . is that they cannot stand wealth." (Quoted in Dean L. Larsen, "Beware Lest Thou Forget the Lord," *Ensign,* May 1991, p. 11.)

The world deems popularity, prosperity, and riches as desirable things. Although in and of themselves these things are not bad, they can alter a person's heart and priorities, which may lead to problems. President Daniel H. Wells, a member of the First Presidency in the early history of the Church, stated, "There will come a time, however, in the history of the Saints, when they will be tried with peace, prosperity, popularity and riches" (in *Journal of Discourses,* 19:367).

Around A.D. 400 the prophet Mormon made a similar observation:

> Yea, and we may see at the very time when he doth prosper his people, yea, in the increase of their fields, their flocks and their herds, and in gold, and in silver, and in all manner of precious things of every kind and art; sparing their lives, and delivering them out of the hands of their enemies; softening the hearts of their enemies that they should not declare wars against them; yea, and in fine, doing all things for the welfare and happiness of his people; yea, then is the time that they do harden their hearts, and do forget the Lord their God, and do trample under their feet the Holy One—yea, and this because of their ease, and their exceedingly great prosperity (Helaman 12:2).

Nephi, a Book of Mormon prophet, saw the last days in a vision. He described a time which for him was yet to come but which for us is a present condition:

> For behold, at that day shall [Satan] rage in the hearts of the children of men, and stir them up to anger against that which is good.

And others will he pacify, and lull them away into carnal security, that they will say: All is well in Zion; yea, Zion prospereth, all is well—and thus the devil cheateth their souls, and leadeth them away carefully down to hell.

. . . Yea, wo be unto him that hearkeneth unto the precepts of men, and denieth the power of God, and the gift of the Holy Ghost! (2 Nephi 28:20–21, 26.)

Nephi saw a people in the latter days who are taken in by worldly influences and who fail to realize what has happened to them. Satan will slowly pacify them into thinking all is well as he envelops them slowly with the philosophies of the world while at the same time subtly persuading them to discount the words of the prophets.

Are we being pacified? Are we hearkening to the precepts of men and denying the power of God? Are we adopting the philosophies of the world while at the same time believing mistakenly that we are following the prophets?

Following are four areas of concern in which the conventional wisdom of the day is in direct opposition to the teachings of the prophets. Will we be found following the prophets' pronouncements, or the world's prominent and prevalent practices? Do we side with revelation or rhetoric?

The Origin of Man

The world teaches that man is an evolutionary product. Over millions of years, through countless mutations and natural selections, man has evolved from lower forms of life to become an intelligent being. This is taught as fact in many high schools and particularly on college and university campuses. Most high school science rooms have charts depicting the evolutionary chain from the trilobites of 550 million years ago, through the dinosaurs of sixty million years ago, to man, who came on the evolutionary scene about one million years ago.

Do the prophets teach this or do they teach something different? Does it matter where man's origin lies? Did God use an evolutionary process to provide bodies for Adam and Eve? The answers can be found in an official statement given by the First Presidency:

> It is held by some that Adam was not the first man upon this earth, and that the original human being was a development from lower orders of the animal creation. These, however, are the theories of men. The word of the Lord declares that Adam was 'the first man of all men' (Moses 1:34), and we are therefore in duty bound to regard him as the primal parent of our race. It was shown to the brother of Jared that all men were created in the *beginning* after the image of God; and whether we take this to mean the spirit or the body, or both, it commits us to the same conclusion: Man began life as a human being, in the likeness of our heavenly Father. (*Improvement Era*, November 1909, p. 80.)

The First Presidency differs from the world. Does it matter that they state, "Man began life as a human being?" Yes, it definitely matters. It matters a great deal. President Marion G. Romney, Second Counselor in the First Presidency in 1973, stated: "That man is a child of God is the most important knowledge available to mortals" ("Man—A Child of God," *Ensign,* July 1973, p. 14). "We mortals are in very deed the literal offspring of God. If men understood, believed, and accepted this truth and lived by it, our sick and dying society would be reformed and redeemed, and men would have peace here and now and eternal joy." (Ibid., p. 11.)

President Romney explains that the idea that man is not the literal offspring of Deity was initially taught by Satan. Adam and Eve "made all things known unto their sons and their daughters. And Satan came among them, saying: 'I am also a son of God; and he commanded them, saying: Believe it not.'" (Moses 5: 12–13.) Elder Boyd K. Packer explains how this teaching can be detrimental to our youth:

Little do we realize what we have brought upon ourselves when we have allowed our children to be taught that man is only an advanced animal. We have compounded the mistake by neglecting to teach moral and spiritual values. Moral laws do not apply to animals for they have no agency. Where there is agency, where there is choice, moral laws must apply. We cannot, absolutely cannot, have it both ways.

When our youth are taught that they are but animals, they feel free, even compelled, to respond to every urge and impulse. We should not be so puzzled at what is happening to society. We have sown the wind, and now we inherit the whirlwind. The chickens, so the saying goes, are now coming home to roost. ("Covenants," *Ensign*, November 1990, p. 85.)

Even with these clear declarations by prophets, some members still try to mix the world's theory of man's origin with revealed doctrine. But the doctrine is clear. The revealed words of the prophets differ from the theories of men. The reasons are given. The choice is ours: revealed religion (the iron rod) from our friends, or worldly wisdom (the spacious building).

Sequence Versus Sensations

President Kimball instructed the youth of the Church about the proper sequence of dating, steady dating, courtship, marriage, schooling, and family. His words are very clear and do not coincide with what the world often encourages:

My beloved young people, you should be serious-minded. Life is not wholly for fun and frolic. It is a most serious business. You will do well to grow up as children, associating with both girls and boys for those first years. When you get in the teen-age years, your social associations should still be general acquaintance with both boys and girls. Any dating or pairing off in social contacts should be postponed until at least the age of 16 or older, and even then there should be much judgment used in selections and in the seriousness.

Young people should still limit the close contacts for several years, since the boy will be going on his mission when he is 19 years old. There should be limited contacts and certainly no approach to the intimate relationships involving sex. There must never be any sex of any kind prior to marriage.

Every boy should have been saving money for his mission and be free from any and all entanglements so he will be worthy. When he is returned from his mission at 21, he should feel free to begin to get acquainted and to date. When he has found the right young woman, there should be a proper temple marriage. One can have all the blessings if he is in control and takes the experiences in proper turn: first some limited social get-acquainted contacts, then his mission, then his courting, then his temple marriage and his schooling and his family, then his life's work. In any other sequence he could run into difficulty.

After marriage young wives should be occupied in bearing and rearing children. I know of no scriptures or authorities which authorize young wives to delay their families or to go to work to put their husbands through college. Young married couples can make their way and reach their educational heights, if they are determined. ("The Marriage Decision," *Ensign,* February 1975, p. 4.)

Some members of the Church rationalize about their standards of pairing off before age sixteen, steady dating too early, or waiting too long to begin a family. Yet our only real choice is between prophets or priestcraft, which is preaching what people want to hear in order to maintain the popularity of the preacher. Priestcraft is condemned by the Lord (see Alma 1:2–17; Helaman 13:26–28).

Sometimes the words of truth given to us by the Lord's prophets are hard medicine to take, but if we will not reject them they will spiritually heal and offer greater rewards than we can see at the present (see 1 Nephi 16:2–3).

The Role of Women

In our modern world of human rights and equal rights, the roles of men and women have been defined and redefined to the point of confusion. Some seem to think that it's demeaning or beneath a woman's dignity to be a homemaker, as demonstrated by the book title *What's a Smart Woman like You Doing at Home?* (Burton, Dittmer, Loveless [Washington, D. C.: Acropolis Books ltd., 1986].) Others demand equality for women in everything, including military service. Equal rights for women have been debated in congress, books, magazines, and TV and radio talk shows for years. What perspective has the Lord given us through our prophets? President Howard W. Hunter explained the role of motherhood in relation to the priesthood: "A man who holds the priesthood has reverence for motherhood. Mothers are given a sacred privilege to 'bear the souls of men; for herein is the work of [the] Father continued, that he may be glorified' (D&C 132:63). The First Presidency has said: 'Motherhood is near to divinity. It is the highest, holiest service to be assumed by mankind' (in James R. Clark, comp., *Messages of the First Presidency,* 6 vols. [Salt Lake City: Bookcraft, 1965–75], 6:178). The priesthood cannot work out its destiny, nor can God's purposes be fulfilled, without our helpmates. Mothers perform a labor the priesthood cannot do." ("Being a Righteous Husband and Father," *Ensign,* November 1994, p. 50.)

Women are equal and in many situations are superior to men, but the roles of men and women differ. The world would sometimes have women take on the roles of men to somehow attempt to make them appear better than or equal with men. This is unwise and unnecessary. President Ezra Taft Benson addressed this idea of equality vs. sameness:

> You were not created to be the same as men. Your natural attributes, affections, and personalities are entirely different from those of a man. They consist of faithfulness, benevolence, kind-

ness, and charity. They give out the personality of a woman. They also balance the more aggressive and competitive nature of a man.

The business world is competitive and sometimes ruthless. We do not doubt that women have both the brainpower and the skills—and in some instances superior abilities—to compete with men. But by competing they must, of necessity, become aggressive and competitive. Thus their godly attributes are diminished and they acquire a quality of sameness with man.

. . . The conventional wisdom of the day would have you be equal with men. We say, we would not have you descend to that level. More often than not the demand for equality means the destruction of the inspired arrangement that God has decreed for man, woman, and the family. Equality should not be confused with equivalence. (*Woman* [Salt Lake City: Deseret Book Co., 1979], p. 71.)

Elder Neal A. Maxwell eloquently commented on the Lord's view of a woman's role in contrast to some statements made by those in the world. He asserts that in the appropriate fulfillment of a woman's role, Christlike attributes are nurtured, which have and will have a profound effect on the world and its history:

So often our sisters comfort others when their own needs are greater than those being comforted. That quality is like the generosity of Jesus on the cross. Empathy during agony is a portion of divinity.

I thank the Father that his Only Begotten Son did not say in defiant protest at Calvary, 'My body is my own!' I stand in admiration of women today who resist the fashion of abortion by refusing to make the sacred womb a tomb!

When the real history of mankind is fully disclosed, will it feature the echoes of gunfire—or the shaping sound of lullabies? The great armistices made by military men—or the peacemaking of women in homes and in neighborhoods? Will what happened in cradles and kitchens prove to be more controlling than what happened in congresses? When the surf of the centuries has made the great pyramids so much sand, the everlasting family will still be

standing, because it is a celestial institution, formed outside telestial time. The women of God know this.

No wonder the men of God support and sustain our sisters in
their unique roles, for the act of deserting home in order to shape
society is like thoughtlessly removing crucial fingers from an im-
periled dike in order to teach people to swim. (Ibid., p. 96.)

One must ask: "Am I like those in Lehi's dream who had par-
taken of the fruit and then hung their heads in shame because of
the pointing fingers of the world?" (See 1 Nephi 8:25.) "Am I at-
tempting to be 'politically correct' to please the world rather than
'prophetically correct' to please the Lord?" "Do I publicly sustain
the prophets but privately wonder if I should be aligning myself
with the current thinking of the world?"

Pro-Choice or Pro-Prophet?

The world uses the euphemism "pro-choice" in reference to
the support of the practice of abortion. Church members should
have no doubts as to what the Church's official position on this
matter is. As reported in the *Church News:*

> To reaffirm the policy of the Church concerning abortion, the
> First Presidency is publishing the following official statement on
> this subject.
>
> "The Church opposes abortion and counsels its members not
> to submit to, be a party to, or perform an abortion except in the
> rare cases where, in the opinion of competent medical counsel, the
> life or health of the woman is seriously endangered or where the
> pregnancy was caused by forcible rape and produces serious emo-
> tional trauma in the victim.
>
> "Even then it should be done only after counseling with the
> bishop or branch president and after receiving divine confirmation
> through prayer.

"Abortion is one of the most revolting and sinful practices in this day, when we are witnessing the frightening evidence of permissiveness leading to sexual immorality." ("Official Statement on Abortion," *Church News*, 5 June 1976, p. 3.)

Elder Russell M. Nelson gave some shocking statistics concerning this practice that is so widely accepted in the world:

A heavy toll on life is included among the evils of war. Data from all nations are appalling. For the United States of America, one hundred thousand were killed in World War I; over four hundred thousand died in World War II. In the first two hundred years as a nation, the lives of over one million Americans were lost due to war.

Regrettable as is the loss of loved ones from war, these figures are dwarfed by the toll of a new war that *annually* claims more casualties than the total number of fatalities from all the wars of this nation.

It is a war on the defenseless—and the voiceless. It is a war on the unborn.

This war, labeled 'abortion,' is of epidemic proportion and is waged globally. Over fifty-five million abortions were reported worldwide in the year 1974 alone. Sixty-four percent of the world's population now live in countries that legally sanction this practice. In the United States of America, over 1.5 million abortions are performed annually. About 25–30 percent of all pregnancies now end in abortion. In some metropolitan areas, there are more abortions performed than live births. Comparable data also come from other nations. ("Reverence for Life," *Ensign*, May 1985, p. 11.)

More statistics sharpen one's sense of horror as to what is being deemed acceptable for many in the world. In an article that asks, "Where did the rest of the class of '91 go?" James W. Huston lists statistics of a magnitude that is hard to comprehend:

Twenty-five percent of the high school graduating class of 1991 are dead.

They died in 1973, the year abortion was made legal. As the remaining 75 percent prepare for their summers after graduation and their futures, they might stop and reflect on the significance of being members of this class.

Vague complaints are heard from the Pentagon and corporate sources that the labor pool seems to be drying up. The number of 18-year-olds is forecast to decrease over the next few years. This seems to come as a surprise to those mentioning the statistics, as if some reverse Baby Boom took place from 1973 on. No mention is made that the primary reason for the decrease in 18-year-olds is that they were aborted 18 years ago.

The number of abortions in this country since 1973, 25 million, exceeds the total populations of Alaska, Arizona, Colorado, Idaho, Iowa, Kansas, Montana, Nebraska, Nevada, New Mexico, North Dakota, Oklahoma, South Dakota, Utah and Wyoming combined.

Why don't we as a society discuss the loss of 10 percent of our population in the last 18 years? If an airplane crashes with 10 people on board, it is national news. But the loss of 1.5 million students from the class of 1991 goes unmentioned, as if to do so is somehow in bad taste. (*AFA Journal,* September 1991, p. 20.)

For the majority of Latter-day Saint youth, abortion is not usually a personal decision they face for themselves. However, many Latter-day Saint youth will have the opportunity to counsel friends who will contemplate abortion. It is the author's hope that Latter-day Saint youth will side with the prophets rather than with the world and, when asked for counsel or an opinion, will be "not ashamed" (Romans 1:16) to declare their allegiance to God's word through his appointed prophets.

Although discussions about abortion often include psychological, physical, financial, and social ramifications, the idea of what God has said is right and wrong through his prophets should not be left out. In the spirit of love and testimony, youth could explain to their peers that the Lord has provided us with prophets who are our friends to guide us in these latter days.

Why Youth Should Listen

The best way to conclude an exhortation to follow the living prophets is to use the words of the prophets themselves to explain why they say what they say and do what they do.

Elder Jeffrey R. Holland:

> So much that we do in this Church is directed toward you, those whom the Book of Mormon calls 'the rising generation' (Mosiah 26:1; Alma 5:49). We who have already walked that portion of life's path that you are now on try to call back to you something of what we have learned. We shout encouragement. We try to warn of pitfalls or perils along the way. Where possible we try to walk with you and keep you close to our side.
>
> . . . The gospel of Jesus Christ marks the only sure and safe path. So older men, seasoned men—men passing on to you the legacy of history—continue to call out to youth. ("Our Priesthood Legacy," *Ensign*, May 1995, p. 38.)

President Boyd K. Packer:

> While you can protect your body from contagious diseases with the proper serum, we cannot immunize our minds and spirits that way. We immunize our minds and our spirits with *ideas*, with *truth*.
>
> It is my purpose to do just that, inoculate you with an idea, a truth, which, if admitted into your thinking and into the cradle of your feelings, may protect you against wicked spiritual diseases to which you are exposed every day of your lives. (Church Educational System young single adult fireside, 7 May 1995.)

Elder Robert D. Hales:

I give my testimony that the prophets of this day have the qualities of the prophets of old and the other prophets of this dispensa-
tion.
    . . . If we listen to the prophets of this day, poverty would be
replaced with loving care for the poor and needy. Many serious
and deadly health problems would be avoided through compli-
ance with the Word of Wisdom and the laws of sexual purity.
Payment of tithing would bless us and we would have sufficient
for our needs. If we follow the counsel given by the prophets, we
can have a life in mortality where we do not bring upon ourselves
unnecessary pain and self-destruction. This does not mean we will
not have challenges. We will. This does not mean we will not be
tested. We will, for this is part of our purpose on earth. But if we
will listen to the counsel of our prophet, we will become stronger
and be able to withstand the tests of mortality. We will have hope
and joy. ("Hear the Prophet's Voice and Obey," *Ensign*, May 1995,
p. 17.)

May we all listen to and heed the words of the Lord's servants—his prophets, our friends—realizing that their voice is
the same as his voice (see D&C 1:38).

*Todd Parker taught seminary for fourteen years and was an instructor
at the LDS institute in Tucson, Arizona, for five years. He is now an
associate professor of Ancient Scripture at Brigham Young University.
He is married to Debra Harbertson, and they have eight children.*

13

BEING FRIENDS WITH JESUS CHRIST

Randal A. Wright

It is very important to have friends in this life. I learned just how important friends were in 1968. Our country was involved in the Vietnam War, so because of the draft the Church had to limit the number of missionaries serving from each ward. I happened to turn nineteen that year, which was the birthday I had looked forward to all my life. Instead of opening a mission call, however, I received the dreaded letter from the government informing me that I had been drafted into the United States Army. How would you feel if this happened to you?

One of my best friends had been killed in the war the year before, so I was very nervous about serving. After eight weeks of basic and advanced training in Texas and California, I was stationed at a large army base that trained infantry soldiers for service in Vietnam. Since I had already completed my training, I was given a private room. This should have been a luxury, but it was devoid of furnishings except for a bed. There were no pictures on the walls, no television, and no radio. Most of the others assigned to help train the infantry soldiers were married and lived off base.

During this time I would go to my assigned duty for eight hours a day and then return to that empty room to stare at the walls and think about home and friends. I was instructed not to associate with any of the soldiers who were in training. With no car, no money, and no friends and isolated from the rest of society, I felt that I was getting a taste of what it would be like to live in hell. I cannot even describe the loneliness and misery I experienced during the months of that assignment. When I first entered the military, the fear of Vietnam was foremost in my mind. After a few weeks of isolation from friends, being sent to Vietnam sounded like a big improvement.

Those three months should not have been so unbearable. I needed friends desperately, but I didn't know where to look. It never occurred to me that I actually had a friend if I only made an effort. Elder Derek A. Cuthbert said, "Everyone needs a friend and everyone has a friend beyond compare—Jesus Christ and him crucified and resurrected for us" ("Our Thirtieth Anniversary as Latter-day Saints," *Ensign*, November 1980, p. 25). Looking back I now see that I missed a wonderful opportunity during those long months to become friends with the greatest friend one could ever hope to have. Being friends with Jesus Christ can be an eternal friendship. Unfortunately, I did not know at the time how to develop that friendship.

Are you friends with the Savior? Do you know how to become his friend? Some realize very early in life that Jesus Christ loves us and is our friend. When my neighbor Shane was on his mission in Plymouth, England, he was asked to speak in sacrament meeting. Before the meeting started, he went to the back of the chapel to spend some quiet time reviewing his talk. A curly-haired five-year-old boy walked up to him and asked, "What's wrong?" Joking with the little boy, he said, "Nobody loves me, and I don't have any friends. That's why I'm sitting back here by myself." The young boy looked up at him very seriously and said, "Jesus loves you." This young boy already realized that Jesus is our friend and that he loves us. If only I had realized that fact during my army days, things would have been much easier.

How can we develop a friendship with Christ? What benefits will come from that friendship? Recently I asked a group of college students to write down the attributes of a true friend. See how many of the following characteristics Christ has.

"I want friends who are loyal and who will stand up for me. A friend is someone who will come to my aid when I'm in trouble."

When I was fifteen, my nonmember friend Johnny and I went to a city recreation area. Walking along, we crossed paths with an older boy I barely knew. He came up to me and challenged me to a fight. Not being as big and as brave as you probably are, I tried to just walk away, but he persisted and began pushing me. He was much bigger than I was, and I was really afraid but I tried to not show it. I tried again to walk away, but he grabbed me and threatened me. What would you do in a similar situation?

I knew my time on earth was short, so I determined that I might as well go down fighting, as much as I was afraid to. Suddenly Johnny was by my side. He told the bully that I was his friend and that he'd better leave me alone. Don't you just love friends like that? But the boy told Johnny to stay out of it and turned back toward me. Before I knew what was happening, Johnny had slugged the older boy, and a fight ensued. Several punches later, the bully was begging for my friend to stop. Now, it's not nice to hit people, but somehow it seemed to be okay that day. I was so humbled that my friend had confronted the bully for me at the risk of his own safety. That experience happened many years ago, but I'll never forget what he did for me. It really helps to have friends who are stronger than you!

My guess is that you have already had many difficult or frightening experiences, both physical and emotional. In times like these, we all need a friend who is very strong. Jesus Christ is that friend. He has all power and will come to the aid of his friends. In the Garden of Gethsemane, he said to the soldiers sent to arrest him, "I am he: if therefore ye seek me, let these go their way" (John 18:8). Another time, he said, "Verily I say unto you my friends, fear not, let your hearts be comforted" (D&C 98:1). With Christ as your friend, there is no need to fear anything that lies before you. He promises: "For I will go before your face. I will be on your right hand and on your left, and my Spirit shall be in your hearts, and mine angels round about you, to bear you up." (D&C 84:88.)

"Good friends correct me in a beneficial way when I'm wrong. When they see me getting off the path, they tell me about it because they care and want me to be my best."

Do you think a real friend would try to tempt you to do anything harmful? Would a real friend say nothing as he watched you make bad choices? No, a real friend wants the best for you and will help you make correct choices in life. As you read the following experience, determine who the newly returned missionary's real friend is.

"The first weekend I was home from my mission, I got together with a group of old friends to go out and talk about the good old times and have some fun. We ended up renting a video, and we returned to a friend's house to watch it. Since I hadn't seen a movie for two years, it never even crossed my mind to ask what the video was rated. I just assumed it would be good, since all the other guys I was with were returned missionaries. When we started watching the movie, my friend's younger sister came in and asked the name of the movie. She was shocked because it was rated R. She then went on to say that it disappointed her that a group of returned missionaries would watch an R-rated movie when the prophets have asked us not to. When this happened, it really hit me hard, and I knew I had to make a decision. I could either continue on the path I was following before my mission, or I could apply what I had learned on my mission and not watch R-rated movies. I decided not to watch R-rated movies ever again. Since then I have received a lot of pressure from friends and fellow students, but I have made a commitment thanks to a twelve-year-old girl."

Who was this man's real friend? Was it the other returned missionaries who were going against the prophets' teachings and encouraging him to do the same? Were his real friends those who pressured him because of his decision not to watch inappropriate movies? Or was his real friend the young girl who had the nerve to correct him when she saw him getting off the safe path? We should never take offense when our friends correct us, because they care about us and want us to be our best. President David O. McKay asked, "If a friend is one who summons us to our best, then is not Jesus Christ our best friend?" (*Gospel Ideals* [Salt Lake City: Improvement Era, 1953], p.145.)

When Christ or his earthly representatives correct us, it is only out of a desire to make us a better person. Joseph Smith was a great man. He was also a friend of Jesus Christ's. Yet even the prophet was chastised by the Lord on several occasions. For example, at one point the Lord rebuked members of the First Presidency for neglecting to teach their families. To the Prophet Joseph, the Lord said, "And now, verily I say unto Joseph Smith, Jun.—You have not kept the commandments, and must needs stand rebuked before the Lord" (D&C 93:47). Would a true friend correct you when you are in the wrong? Of course he or she would. They want you to improve your life and will help you along that path. Elder Marvin J. Ashton said, "I bear you my witness that our Lord and Savior, Jesus Christ, is our friend. In his loving processes of command, rebuke, greeting, revelation, encouragement, and long-suffering, he daily proves this. Certainly he is willing to take us the way we are, but he wants to leave us improved in his word and his paths." ("What Is a Friend?" *Ensign,* January 1973, p. 43.) A real friend will do whatever is necessary to help you become a better person, including pointing out when you are choosing the wrong path.

"A good friend knows your faults, strengths, fears, and dreams and loves you anyway. They don't necessarily look at how you are, but how you can be. There are no ulterior motives or agendas with true friends, just unconditional love. A good friend would sacrifice personal interests or even safety to help you."

Years ago I taught early-morning seminary in southeast Texas. It was not easy having a full-time job, serving on the stake high council, and teaching five mornings a week starting at 5:55 A.M. Some of you will have that assignment in the future. There were several mornings when I was not prepared as well as I should have been. There were times when I was afraid to stand in front of the class. But those seminary students accepted me as I was and became my friends.

On one occasion, I mentioned that my cousin Ned was getting married in the Los Angeles Temple. Knowing that Ned had been my good friend growing up, someone asked if I was going to his wedding. I replied that I would love to go, but I had to give a talk and sing that weekend and I couldn't afford it anyway. Several weeks later, I walked into the classroom and the students wanted me to play a game. I went throughout the building looking for clues they'd hidden. Back in our classroom, I was instructed to pull the curtains back and read what was written on the chalkboard. I didn't fully grasp the meaning of the message at first. It said:

> Put on your rags,
> And shine your shoes.
> Grab your bags.
> We've got good news.

> We canceled your talk
> And also your song.
> You're going to L.A.—
> But not for too long.
>
> You need to go home
> So you can get ready,
> For later this evening
> You will see Neddie!
>
> We love you!
> The Seniors of '85

Taped to the board was an envelope that the students encouraged me to open. Inside I found two plane tickets to L.A. These students had saved their money (including lunch money) to buy me a ticket to attend my cousin's wedding. I will never forget the love shown. They overlooked the days I had come to class unprepared; they loved me and sacrificed for me despite my faults. They truly followed the Savior's admonition, "This is my commandment, That ye love one another, as I have loved you" (John 15:12).

A willingness to sacrifice is the ultimate expression of love. That is why Christ should be considered our greatest friend. He said: "Greater love hath no man than this, that a man lay down his life for his friends" (John 15:13).

President Howard W. Hunter explained what Christ went through: "Think of it! When [the Lord's] body was taken from the cross and hastily placed in a borrowed tomb, he, the sinless Son of God, had already taken upon him not only the sins and temptations of every human soul who will repent, but all of our sickness and grief and pain of every kind. He suffered these afflictions as we suffer them, according to the flesh. He suffered them all. He did this to perfect his mercy and his ability to lift us above every earthly trial." (See Alma 7:11–12.) ("He Is Risen," *Ensign,* May 1988, pp.16–17.)

"A friend is someone who has qualities that I would like to develop in myself. They stand up for what they believe in and are an example for me in things that are right."

Recently I had the opportunity of teaching a class of prospective seminary teachers. One of the students was a college football player who, at six feet eight inches and 335 pounds, was projected to go high in the NFL draft, which of course would mean a huge salary and much prestige. However, before the draft took place he sent letters to all the NFL teams informing them that he had made a decision not to play professional football. Although he had always dreamed of playing pro football, his mission had changed his priorities. One of his major concerns was that he did not want to play on Sunday. Many people thought it was wrong to give up the money and fame that comes with this prestigious occupation. Because he chose to follow his values, he will forego his boyhood dreams and become a teacher. I told him that he would never know what his example had done for me. Because of the courage and dedication of this young man, I want to be a better person. He gave me a greater desire to stand up for what I believe in, even when it is hard.

If true friends set a good example for us to follow, then Jesus Christ is the greatest friend we can ever have. To the Nephites, he said: "Therefore I would that ye should be perfect even as I, or your Father who is in heaven is perfect" (3 Nephi 12:48). Jesus Christ lived a perfect life. Since he committed no sins in his life, he is able to say to his friends, "Follow me." Elder Sterling W. Sill said, "The most inspiring thing about the life of Jesus was not his ability to quiet the storm or control the tempest, but absolute control of himself" (in Conference Report, October 1963, p. 78).

"A true friend is someone who loves me in spite of my imperfections. A true friend forgives me when one of my imperfections or weaknesses has offended him or her."

Elder Richard G. Scott said that if you will make the effort, "you will also discover the greatest friend of all, Jesus the Christ, our Savior and Redeemer, full of perfect love and boundless compassion, with the power to forgive and forget" ("We Love You—Please Come Back," *Ensign,* May 1986, p. 12).

"Life is full of challenges, disappointments, and discouragement. A friend will comfort me when I'm down and discouraged."
Years ago I was the chairman of the first big festival our city had ever attempted. I wanted it to succeed more than anything, since I was the one who had proposed the idea to the chamber of commerce. There were beauty pageants, 10-K races, cook-offs, a carnival, food booths, displays, and entertainment. The biggest event planned, however, was a concert by a famous country-western band to be held in an outdoor stadium. Many people worked hundreds of hours to make the event special for our community.

The opening day of the festival came, and large crowds began to arrive. And then it happened. A huge storm blew in, and it rained and rained. The crowds left, the booths closed, and the concert had to be canceled. All the work we had put in went down the drain. The money collected from the sale of concert tickets had to be refunded, but we still had to pay the band half of their money. I was so upset I just went home and lay on my bed and cried. My wife, Wendy, who is the best friend I have on earth, came in and sat on the bed by me and told me how proud she was of me for putting the festival together. She comforted me and told me that it would all work out and that she loved me. Just hearing her words and feeling her support made things better. From that disastrous beginning, the festival is now in its fifteenth year.

In mortal life, you and I will have many challenges to face. Sometimes the burden will be heavy. It is during these trying times that we should turn to Jesus Christ, who is "our best friend, who clears up all our doubts. He heals our wounds and turns our pain into sweet experiences." (Horacio A. Tenorio, "Teachings of a Loving Father," *Ensign,* May 1990, p. 80.)

To those whose lives are full of challenges, disappointment, and discouragement, the Savior said: "Come unto me, all ye that labour and are heavy laden, and I will give you rest. Take my yoke upon you, and learn of me; for I am meek and lowly in heart: and ye shall find rest unto your souls. For my yoke is easy, and my burden is light." (Matthew 11:28–30.)

"A true friend is someone who wants to be with me and is excited to see me after an absence."

When our son returned from his mission to North Carolina, we went to the Salt Lake airport to pick him up. It was a great experience to be reunited with someone we love so much. You have probably enjoyed similar experiences in your life.

When Christ visited the righteous Nephites, another glorious reunion took place. After being with them, he told them that he needed to go to the Father and then to visit the lost tribes of Israel. "And it came to pass that when Jesus had thus spoken, he cast his eyes round about again on the multitude, and beheld they were in tears, and did look steadfastly upon him as if they would ask him to tarry a little longer with them. And he said unto them: Behold, my bowels are filled with compassion towards you." (3 Nephi 17:5–6.)

During this time, Christ healed the sick and blessed the children and wept with the multitude because of the love he had for these friends. The whole mission of Jesus Christ is to bring souls back to the celestial kingdom so that we can be an eternal family.

My students pointed out many other qualities that they look for in a true friend. In every case, Jesus Christ meets the requirements to be our best friend. We need his friendship. He pleads for ours. With Jesus Christ as our friend, we will be able to face every challenge and withstand every temptation. Elder Malcolm S. Jeppsen pointed out: "Just think! With Jesus as your friend, you may receive increased strength and testimony that will uphold you against temptations when they arise." ("Who Is a True Friend?" *Ensign,* May 1990, p. 45.)

Looking back at my teenage years, I would have given anything to have Christ as my friend. Unfortunately, I did not know how to develop that relationship. How do we become friends with Jesus Christ?

It Takes Effort

It takes effort to gain and maintain a friendship. My friend Tom has a little girl who wanted a cat. He took her to the animal shelter and told her to pick one out. She saw a beautiful cat and walked over to pick it up. But as she reached down, the cat quickly ran away from her and hid. So she picked out a second one that was not quite as beautiful as the first. As she approached, it hissed loudly at her. While she was looking around, another cat came up to her and began to rub against her leg. It was by far the most unattractive of the three. Which one do you think she picked to take home with her that day? The first two cats could have gone home to a life of luxury and love, but they rejected the very person who would have gladly provided it for them. It took a little effort on their part, but they were not willing to give it.

Jesus Christ wants to be our friend and provide us the luxury and love that his friendship can offer. He said, "Behold, I stand at the door, and knock: if any man hear my voice, and open the door, I will come in to him, and will sup with him, and he with me" (Revelation 3:20). It is up to us to open that door. When he comes knocking, we can't run away and hide. We can't hiss and act like we don't want him around. We must make an effort to be his friend. Shortly before his crucifixion, Jesus told his disciples how to be his friend: "Ye are my friends, if ye do whatsoever I command you" (John 15:14). Such a simple request, yet so few of us are willing to put forth the effort to open the door and invite him in. For those who keep the commandments, a great friendship develops.

I've noticed that once we have a friend, it takes effort to keep the relationship alive. When we moved to Utah from Texas, our oldest daughter left many good friends behind. It was not easy for her. I wondered if she would be able to maintain those friendships over time. Much to my surprise, she has. How did she do it? Maybe it was the letters and phone calls over the years. Maybe the pictures of her friends in her room helped also. She put forth a lot of effort to maintain those friendships. Now, four years later, we are moving back to Texas. Those same friends are looking forward to a great reunion.

Jesus Christ has written letters to us: they are called the scriptures. In these letters he gives us his encouragement and love. When was the last time you read his letters? We don't call our brother Jesus Christ directly, but we can call on our Father through prayer in his name and feel his presence in our life.

Of course, we need pictures to remember our friends, so we should all have a picture of Christ in our room to remind us of him. Recently I met a teenaged girl in Toronto, Canada, named Sunny, who told me of an experience she had at school. She read an article in the *New Era* about a young woman who hung a picture of Christ in her school locker. Sunny was so impressed with the story that she decided to do the same. Her locker partner was not a Latter-day Saint, so Sunny asked her for permission, which she granted. The first day the picture was up, Sunny began hearing comments from other students whose lockers were close to hers. In the following days the number of students gathering around grew larger and larger. Many of their comments were negative, and some used the Lord's name in vain. Sunny heard a boy say to a large crowd gathered around, "You see, I told you she had a picture of Christ in her locker." She told me that many of the boys had pornographic pictures in their lockers, yet no one said anything to them.

Soon the picture was drawing so much attention that Sunny decided it wasn't worth having it up and that she was going to remove it. But when she started to take it down, her locker mate asked her what she was doing. Sunny said, "It's not worth it. There are so many people gathered around our locker making rude comments that I'm going to take it down." Her friend then said, "Please don't take it down. Ever since you put that picture up, I have wanted to be a better person. In fact, I never want to do anything wrong now because I know that Jesus Christ will be looking at me when I open my locker!" She had become friends with Christ just by looking at his picture every day. That new friendship had changed her life.

Every week we have another very special way to remember our friend: the sacrament. During this sacred time, we are each given a chance to ponder our friendship with the Savior. In the prayer recited by ordained priesthood holders, we are told to "always remember him and keep his commandments which he has given them" (D&C 20:77).

It takes effort to make and maintain friendships, but the effort will bring eternal benefits. We show our friendship with Christ by how we treat others. He gave his life for all of us; it makes no difference whether we are black or white, rich or poor. If he had been willing to extend his friendship only to people like himself, he would have been alone, and we would have no chance for exaltation. We should imitate him in loving others and allowing for differences between them and us the way Christ does.

Michelle had once been active in the Church, but she became heavily involved in inappropriate activities and quit coming to church. On the other hand, Linda had always been active and always did what was right. Following is a letter that Linda wrote to Michelle to persuade her to come back to church.

Dear Michelle,

How are you doing? You're probably wondering why I'm writing. Well, it's because *I miss you.* I remember all the fun times we've had over the years. Michelle, you are a very special friend to me and all the other girls. No one told me to write this. This isn't an assignment or anything like that. This is a letter to a wonderful person I miss dearly. I love you so much and so does everyone else. I know that our Heavenly Father and his son Jesus Christ love you also. I'm not trying to preach to you; I'm trying to tell you how I truly feel. Again, I love you and I'll always be here for you. Call me anytime from anywhere to talk.

> Love always,
> Linda

Because of friends like Linda, Michelle eventually came back into the Church and married in the temple. I believe Linda strengthened her friendship with Christ by making the effort to bring a soul back to him. By keeping the commandments, we make friends with Christ on earth and continue that friendship in the eternities. The reward will be a glorious reunion in the next life with a dear friend. Melvin J. Ballard described what that reunion would be like:

> I found myself one evening in the dreams of the night, in that sacred building, the Temple. After a season of prayer and rejoicing, I was informed that I should have the privilege of entering into one of those rooms, to meet a glorious Personage, and as I entered the door, I saw, seated on a raised platform, the most glorious Being my eyes ever have beheld, or that I ever conceived existed in all the eternal worlds. As I approached to be introduced, he arose and stepped towards me with extended arms, and he smiled as he softly spoke my name. If I shall live to be a million years old, I shall never forget that smile. He took me into his arms and kissed me, pressed me to His bosom, and blessed me, until the marrow of my bones seemed to melt! When He had finished, I fell at His feet, and as I bathed them with my tears and kisses, I saw the prints of the nails in the feet of the Redeemer of the world. The feeling that I had in the presence of Him who hath all things in his hands, to have His love, His affection, and His blessings was such that if I ever can receive that of which I had but a foretaste, I would give all that I am, all that I ever hope to be, to feel what I then felt! (Bryant S. Hinckley, *The Faith of Our Pioneer Fathers* [Salt Lake City: Bookcraft, 1956], pp. 226–27.)

Randal A. Wright *earned his Ph.D. in family studies from Brigham Young University and is the director of the Austin, Texas, Institute of Religion. He is a frequent speaker at Especially for Youth, Education Week, and Know Your Religion programs. He and his wife, Wendy, have five children.*